New Directions for
Higher Education

Martin Kramer and
Judith Block McLaughlin
CO-EDITORS-IN-CHIEF

Lessons Learned from Virtual Universities

Katrina A. Meyer

EDITOR

Number 146 • Summer 2009
Jossey-Bass
San Francisco

LESSONS LEARNED FROM VIRTUAL UNIVERSITIES
Katrina A. Meyer (ed.)
New Directions for Higher Education, no. 146
Martin Kramer, Judith Block McLaughlin, Co-Editors-in-Chief

Microfilm copies of issues and articles are available in 16mm and 35mm, as well as microfiche in 105mm, through University Microfilms Inc., 300 North Zeeb Road, Ann Arbor, MI 48106-1346.

NEW DIRECTIONS FOR HIGHER EDUCATION (ISSN 0271-0560, electronic ISSN 1536-0741) is part of The Jossey-Bass Higher and Adult Education Series and is published quarterly by Wiley Subscription Services, Inc., A Wiley Company, at Jossey-Bass, 989 Market Street, San Francisco, CA 94103-1741. Periodicals Postage Paid at San Francisco, California, and at additional mailing offices. POSTMASTER: Send address changes to New Directions for Higher Education, Jossey-Bass, 989 Market Street, San Francisco, CA 94103-1741.

New Directions for Higher Education is indexed in Current Index to Journals in Education (ERIC); Higher Education Abstracts.

SUBSCRIPTIONS cost $89 for individuals and $228 for institutions, agencies, and libraries. See ordering information page at end of journal.

EDITORIAL CORRESPONDENCE should be sent to the Co-Editors-in-Chief, Martin Kramer, 2807 Shasta Road, Berkeley, CA 94708-2011 and Judith Block McLaughlin, Harvard GSE, Gutman 435, Cambridge, MA 02138.

Cover photograph © Digital Vision

www.josseybass.com

CONTENTS

EDITOR'S NOTES

It is likely that you have heard about "virtual universities." It is just as likely that you have an opinion about virtual universities. But what do you really know about them? Beyond the hype and the statements of supporters and critics, what are they? What do they do? And how do they do it?

The purpose of this *New Directions for Higher Education* monograph is to answer these questions by presenting the first collection of research on virtual universities (VUs). These chapters are from individuals with experience working in or studying VUs, based on surveys, evaluations, and data. You will find support for the VU phenomenon among these authors, but you will also find a clear-headed understanding of the challenges VUs face in the future.

We expect that such research may be interesting on its own and useful to other virtual institutions. But this monograph also emphasizes the lessons for traditional institutions to be drawn from the experiences of VUs. Its scope attempts to be comprehensive, or as comprehensive as we can make it at this time. The truth is that VUs have been operational for only a short time—since 1995, when the Western Governors began talking of a virtual university. Although nearly every state has eventually had one or more, higher education's experience with these new phenomena is still relatively young. However, despite our short experience with VUs, they have grown to be an accepted part of the higher education landscape, and they have also subtly changed that landscape, making online learning and online ways of doing business more acceptable among traditional higher education institutions.

All of the VUs included in this monograph are located in the United States, and all but one are or have been funded in part by state governments. In this way, this research captures only one form and type of VU. It is important to remember that the United States is not the only incubator of VUs, and many others exist in other countries. However, for the purpose of this monograph we have narrowed our focus to mostly state-funded or -initiated VUs.

Even though there is more variability in VUs than can be covered in an effort of this size, this monograph focuses on the research and careful analysis of several kinds of virtual organization: single institution and consortia, lower division only and all levels, single state or multistate, and an international import. The focus on organizations and the new and evolving models for virtual institutions distinguishes this monograph from other works on virtual education. It attempts to determine whether VUs have fulfilled the lofty goals of advocates—or the suspicions of critics.

Each chapter contributes a view on the VU phenomenon. Chapter One, by James Cox, presents an overview of the first and most comprehensive survey of public virtual universities in the United States. Because Epper and Garn (2003) serves as a benchmark for all studies on VUs, it seemed necessary to include a short summary for the reader.

Chapter Two reviews several new definitions and taxonomies developed to help categorize and understand VUs. This chapter, by Katrina Meyer, will certainly stretch the reader's understanding of what a VU is, given that it can have many forms.

With Chapter Three, the monograph begins to focus on individual VUs. In "Lessons Learned from WashingtonOnline," Connie Broughton discusses the experience of WAOL as it was designed by the Washington State Community and Technical Colleges, and how it subsequently evolved.

Chapter Four maintains a focus on lower-division virtual education by covering the development of the University System of Georgia's eCore program. Libby V. Morris and Catherine Finnegan discuss both successes and challenges resulting from the program's initial design and assumptions.

With Chapter Five, the monograph tackles the first well-known VU, the Western Governors University. Katrina Meyer discusses her research on WGU's early development and change in focus.

Haixia Xu and Libby V. Morris compare three state-level virtual universities in Chapter Six: Kentucky Virtual University, Ohio Learning Network, and UT TeleCampus. This comparison focuses on differences but also some initial conclusions on what worked and what did not.

Chapter Seven compares four state-level virtual universities: California Virtual University, Florida Virtual Campus, Michigan Virtual University, and Kentucky Virtual University. Myk Garn chronicles their development and changes and assesses the impact on other institutions in each state.

All of the VUs chronicled so far are still in operation, but it is important to include an example of a VU that failed. Chapter Eight, by Lynette Krenelka, is a case study of the short life of U.S. Open University, which began, ran, and folded in a mere four years.

Chapter Nine offers an overview of a recent study on how current VUs in the United States and Canada are funded. Russell Poulin and Demarée Michelau discuss some initial conclusions on the success of different funding models.

Chapter Ten outlines a model for integrating student services—and specifically academic advising—into the world of VUs. Written by George Steele and Karen Thurmond, the model integrates cognitive theories and technology uses for a comprehensive look at how online academic advising ought to occur.

From interviews with VU leaders, Karen Vignare reports on original research, conducted for this monograph. Chapter Eleven outlines the interviewees' key guidelines for institutions contemplating a VU.

NEW DIRECTIONS FOR HIGHER EDUCATION • DOI: 10.1002/he

Chapter Twelve identifies what we know and do not know about VUs. Katrina Meyer identifies the research questions we need to have answered and invites other researchers to undertake research on these fascinating, confounding, and still largely misunderstood institutions.

The aim of the monograph is to inform students of higher education about the VU phenomenon, and to do so through research studies. It is also intended to stimulate graduate students to tackle research on issues of importance to VUs and virtual education, so that new researchers can be added to the ranks of higher education faculty with an interest in this field. It is also hoped that higher education faculty who teach about governance, funding, and policy may wish to add research on VUs to their existing classes. Perhaps faculty whose research interests and expertise in funding, organizational models, governance, and policy will be stimulated to focus their research on VUs and their various models, thereby adding to our understanding of how VUs and traditional institutions are different, or similar, or both. Lastly, it is hoped that higher education leaders—at the institution, system, and government levels—will better understand these new types of institution, be better able to develop policy and plans for them, and find some useful practices for implementation at traditional institutions.

Katrina A. Meyer
Editor

Reference

Epper, R. M., and Garn, M. *Virtual College and University Consortia: A National Study.* Boulder, Colo.: State Higher Education Executive Officers, 2003.

KATRINA A. MEYER is associate professor of higher and adult education at the University of Memphis.

1

A summary of the Epper and Garn (2003) study of virtual universities in the United States.

Background: What the States Created

James C. Cox

Prior to 2003, virtual universities were being created at a rate that would question the usual perception that higher education rarely changed, or changed (if at all) at a glacial speed. No comprehensive study of what was actually being created had been done; nor had anyone tapped the experiences of the developers in the states to see what was working and what was not. To begin to understand what happened in the rush to create virtual organizations, the State Higher Education Executive Officers and the Western Cooperative for Educational Telecommunications undertook a study in 2002 that would identify the types of organizational and financial models in use; the statewide goals that virtual colleges or universities (VCUs) were created to meet (and how they may have changed); the policies, programs, and student participation for VCUs; and implications for policymakers. Epper and Garn (2003) produced the final report for this nationwide study.

An Overview of VCUs in 2002

Epper and Garn (2003) found that forty-five states had created sixty-one VCUs that were consortia involving several institutions (p. 13). When asked who or what organization initiated the VCU, 49 percent gave credit to higher education institutions, 29 percent said the system governing board and another 28 percent said the state coordinating or governing board, 12 percent gave credit to the legislature, and another 12 percent gave it to the governor. Clearly, multiple actors were involved in some states.

The majority (61 percent) of VCUs include both two- and four-year institutions, fifteen (25 percent) include only two-year institutions, and nine

New Directions for Higher Education, no. 146, Summer 2009 © Wiley Periodicals, Inc.
Published online in Wiley InterScience (www.interscience.wiley.com) • DOI: 10.1002/he.340

(15 percent) include four-year institutions. Only sixteen (26 percent) include private, not-for-profit institutions and seven (11 percent) include high school partners. It is important to note that with the passage of time current figures are likely different.

Nearly half (49 percent) of the VCUs offered certificate programs, 58.8 percent offered associate degrees, 43.1 percent offered bachelor's degrees, 43.1 percent offered master's degrees, and 9.8 percent offered doctoral degrees. Sixteen of the VCUs served high school students, eight furnished adult education or GED courses, thirty-four served undergraduates, twenty-one served graduate students, and another twelve offered noncredit continuing education. To deliver these programs, all of the VCUs used online resources, 56.9 percent used compressed video, 33.3 percent used satellite, 43.1 percent used cable, 35.3 percent used correspondence study, 15.7 percent used classroom, and 11.8 percent used a traveling teacher. Of the 23 VCUs that reported information on enrollment, 240,188 students were enrolled during fall 2002, with an average enrollment of 10,443. As for completion rates, only 29 percent do the tracking, with rates falling within the 70–90 percent range. The highest completion rate reported was 96 percent.

States were consistent in their reasons for founding virtual colleges and universities, primarily to increase access to higher education to the underserved or those at a distance. However, since their inception, the institutions' missions and goals have evolved to include addressing emerging concerns of states such as improving efficiency and meeting state workforce needs. When asked to assess the VCUs' success in meeting specific goals, 47.1 percent of the respondents felt they had expanded access, 39.2 percent had furnished one-stop shopping for higher education courses, 37.3 percent fostered collaborative development, 37.3 percent offered statewide faculty development, and 35.3 percent developed new courses and programs. Other goals (such as creating a better-educated workforce or increasing economic development) were evaluated least.

Epper and Garn (2003) also found that most VCUs were started directly or indirectly with state appropriations. Ten VCUs received an initial capitalization of more than $1 million, nine received between $500,000 and $1 million, and ten more received less than $500,000. Member institutions paid a variety of fees (which differ with the consortium) but include paying regular dues, service fees, or a start-up fee. In many cases, staff were reassigned or donated to the effort by member institutions. However, there was evidence to suggest the VCUs are becoming financially self-reliant. Twelve VCUs were self-supporting and another eleven reported plans to become self-supporting. Specifically, decentralized VCUs appeared to have become more self-supporting. Epper and Garn (2003) attributed this to the need for decentralized VCUs to generate funds to operate. The less the state appropriation was, the greater the reliance on tuition and other sources of revenue to fund VCUs.

VCUs also played a vital role in policy development and implementation. As a matter of fact, Epper and Garn (2003) noted that the majority of

VCUs studied were expected to be players in the development of policies for member institutions. Usually, governing boards and state legislatures determine policies for institutions of higher learning with little or no input from institutions. Epper and Garn found that centralized VCUs were more likely than decentralized VCUs to be involved in policy change and development.

Organizational Models Compared

Although initially VCUs were created in many forms, Epper and Garn (2004a; 2004b) found that four models for consortia had emerged: the distributed agency model, distributed enterprise model, central agency model, and central enterprise model. This taxonomy is based on Wolf and Johnstone (1999), which is discussed in Chapter Two.

The *distributed agency model*, which was usually located within an academic agency such as a governing board, offered limited service and was not highly centralized within an institution. Institutions with this model usually supplied the electronic course catalog and were successful in decreasing program duplication. The *distributed enterprise model* had many of the same features as the distributed agency model, but it furnished some business functions such as quality control assurance, benchmarking, and assessment. The *central agency model* was highly centralized within an institution and offered assistance with articulation and student-related services. Centralizing resources and implementing technological initiatives were two of the major characteristics associated with the central agency model. However, there were few or no business-related functions within the central agency model. The *central enterprise model* was the only one that had strong business practices and was highly centralized. This particular model produced revenue for the institution by focusing on efficiencies, standardization, assessment, and benchmarking. Over the years, each model gradually developed its own identity, but by 2003 the existing VCUs were falling into two main—and distinctly different—models: centralized and decentralized (or distributed).

Centralized and decentralized VCUs had some common features: online course catalog, help desks, marketing, training for faculty and staff, and proctoring services. However, centralized VCUs generally provided services to students such as a bookstore and online services (registration, library, applications). Centralized VCUs also usually had larger staffs than decentralized VCUs (although one can presume that the participating institutions contributed staff to the effort, which is difficult to account for). Administrators (senior level, administrative support, IT, instructional design) increased from founding the VCU to the time of the survey. One of the most striking findings in the Epper and Garn (2003) study was the shift in course design staff from full-time to part-time. This may capture larger processes under way in the VCU where a service was gradually moved to the participating institutions. In 2002, distributed VCUs had 9.0 staff (3.5 full-time and 5.4 part-time), while centralized VCUs had 21.4 staff (14.0 full-time and 7.4 part-time). In any case, VCUs were not becoming huge organizations.

There were also differences in enrollment data, degree programs offered, and funding for centralized and decentralized VCUs. Epper and Garn (2003) noted that it was sometimes difficult to assess whether the majority of students enrolled in VCUs were from campus-based or distant locations. More than half (52 percent) reported that enrolled students were at a physical distance; 42 percent of VCUs claimed that their primary users were campus-based. Furthermore, the majority of students who attended centralized VCUs were from campus-based locations, and the majority of students attending decentralized VCUs were more likely to serve students from distant locations. Centralized VCUs were more likely than decentralized VCUs to gather and report enrollment data.

Decentralized VCUs offered more degree programs than centralized VCUs. This phenomenon was due in large part to decentralized VCU's ability to use several institutions within a state to offer degrees. Whereas centralized VCUs offered fewer degree programs but provided greater academic and student services to those enrolled, the primary modes of course delivery for both decentralized and centralized VCUs were online, compressed video, cable, and correspondence.

Lessons Learned

Lessons learned from the research conducted on VCUs and the experiences of the developers may be helpful for traditional institutions that wish to innovate. In particular, Epper and Garn (2004a) cited several lessons learned from VCUs that can be advantageous to higher education. For example, VCUs that operate with a business model, not an educational one, had greater success in meeting their goals. This does not argue for traditional institutions to cast aside their educational goals; it does imply that some attention to business goals may be warranted.

Also, VCUs that were centralized outperformed institutions that were decentralized. Epper and Garn (2004a) noted centralized VCUs were successful because they focused on more global issues such as standardizing courses, benchmarking with other VCUs, and assessing and evaluating goals. Furthermore, centralized VCUs were better funded than decentralized institutions. Again, this finding implies that centralizing some functions seems to have laudatory outcomes, and if these outcomes are valuable to traditional institutions, then perhaps moving some activities toward a more centralized model may be valuable to them.

Epper and Garn (2003) found that most VCUs began by placing their general education or core curriculum online. Once the VCUs became efficient with the general curriculum, they tackled more complicated courses and issues. This could prove beneficial to higher education institutions across the nation to decrease the cost associated with general education or core curricula. By learning how to do online learning well on core courses, the lessons can be easily transferred to other courses or taught to faculty interested in teaching online in an effective manner.

In addition, VCUs that received less state appropriations found other ways to generate revenue to pay for expenses. As state appropriations become smaller sources of revenues for postsecondary education, colleges and universities will need to find creative ways to generate revenue and reduce expenses: "Today VCUs appear to be emphasizing goals more attuned to state/system higher education efficiency as well as meeting state workforce needs and emphasizing less the traditional (access and underserved) goals of distance education" (Epper and Garn, 2003, p. 35). Given the likelihood that state funding for higher education will be affected by state economies, the experience of VCUs in finding new revenue streams and streamlining costs may be helpful to all higher education institutions. It might be useful for colleges and universities across the nation to study VCUs and implement some of their practices, especially their business practices, in an effort to address societal needs and be more efficient with scarce resources. However, it is important to note that the higher the funding level, the better the VCU felt it could meet its goals. In other words, funding does matter, although where the funding comes from is likely to shift in the days ahead.

VCUs have been characterized as the "lubricant needed for a massive shifting of the gears in higher education" (Epper and Garn 2003, p. 7), which may be passing or only hitting its maximum need. Perhaps the answer to this conundrum is whether and to what extent traditional institutions have shifted those gears. Perhaps VCUs will continue because lubrication of gears is needed and because new shifts must be made.

Finally, VCUs evolved and changed their services on the basis of emerging needs of students and their constituent institutions. Perhaps this is the most important lesson for traditional institutions from the VCU experience: change seems to continue to happen, shifting what is needed for students to succeed, services to pay for themselves, and structures to improve and operate ever more efficiently. And change continues.

References

Epper, R. M., and Garn, M. *Virtual College and University Consortia: A National Study*. Boulder, Colo.: State Higher Education Executive Officers, 2003.

Epper, R. M., and Garn, M. "The Virtual University in America: Lessons from Research and Experience." *EDUCAUSE Center for Applied Research Bulletin*, 2004a. Retrieved Dec. 31, 2008, from http://net.educause.edu/ir/library/pdf/ERB0402.pdf.

Epper, R. M., and Garn, M. "Virtual Universities: Real Possibilities." *EDUCAUSE Review*, 2004b, *39*(2), 28–39. Retrieved Dec. 31, 2008, from http://net.educause.edu/ir/library/pdf/ERM0422.pdf.

Wolf, D. B., and Johnstone, S. M. "Cleaning up the Language: Establishing a Consistent Vocabulary for Electronically Delivered Academic Programs." *Change, 31*(4), July/August 1999, 34–39.

JAMES C. COX is a doctoral candidate in higher and adult education at the University of Memphis.

2

This chapter provides new definitions or descriptors for different types of virtual universities that have been proposed by several authors.

New Definitions for New Higher Education Institutions

Katrina A. Meyer

New terms were exploding early in the development of distance learning and virtual universities. Distance learning, online learning, e-learning, and distributed learning were applied to the various new forms of learning using online or Web-based materials and processes. However, largely thanks to the immediate popularity of the Western Governors' use of "virtual university," the term was applied to a variety of organizational types that were very different from one another. This was (and still is) confusing to many both within and outside academe, and it led to a rash of misunderstandings about what "virtual" meant and what a virtual university might do.

What was a virtual university (VU)? The period of the 1990s was rife with new organizations, new forms of collaboration, and so-called virtual universities formed by institutions and states wanting to enter what was perceived at the time as a growing and lucrative marketplace. Although several organizations called themselves VUs, they often did not look or operate anything like other VUs. What was needed was some clarity in the terms used and help getting our arms around the new organizational types being developed to address the growing need for distance learning.

Seven Organizational Models

Hanna (1998) developed seven emerging organizational models that were compared to the "traditional" university. The traditional university was characterized by a residential student body, a geographic service area from which the

NEW DIRECTIONS FOR HIGHER EDUCATION, no. 146, Summer 2009 © Wiley Periodicals, Inc.
Published online in Wiley InterScience (www.interscience.wiley.com) • DOI: 10.1002/he.341

majority of students were drawn, full-time faculty members, a central library and physical plant, nonprofit financial status, and an orientation to evaluation that stressed inputs (such as incoming student characteristics, library holdings, faculty-student ratios) rather than outputs (such as student learning).

Extended traditional universities are traditional universities that offer select programs for primarily nonresident adults. This arrangement does not question the basic arrangements of the parent university but is isolated within a continuing education or extension division. Numerous examples of such arrangements exist as many institutions now offer online programs to students located at a distance from the institution.

For-profit adult-centered universities derive the majority of their revenue from tuition paid by students or their employers and focuses on programs that draw large numbers of students, such as business, IT skills, and education. For-profit universities also tend to develop standardized curricula, use adjunct faculty, and offer basic student services (no football teams or exercise labs). The University of Phoenix is perhaps the best example of this organizational model, although Strayer, ITT Technical Institutes, DeVry, and Sylvan Learning Systems are additional examples.

Distance education/technology-based universities use a number of technologies to offer learning and services to students. They are also oriented to serving adults with their workforce needs but offer instruction of various lengths rather than only degree programs. Hanna (1998) separates this category into three subcategories. The first one developed from a *correspondence tradition* that used conventional print-based courses distributed by mail. Examples of these institutions are the British Open University and Athabasca University in Canada. The second subcategory developed from an *extended classroom tradition* and used various technologies such as satellite or two-way video and audio systems to extend on-campus face-to-face instruction to students at distant sites, as with the National Technological University. The third subcategory is *emerging online Web-based universities,* developed to use online technologies exclusively.

Corporate universities are units of corporations offering education and training tailored to the specific needs of the corporation. This includes McDonald's University, Motorola University, and Disney University.

University-industry strategic alliances are partnerships between and among organizations with particular strengths. These alliances may include universities and private companies or only private companies that pool resources drawing on the organizations' specialized content or technologies.

Degree/certification competency-based organizations take advantage of advancement in competency-based learning and the assessment of student learning. Regents College and Western Governors University are examples of this type of organization.

Global multinational universities have been created to address global needs for education, as with the Global Alliance for Transnational

Education. Hanna (1998) notes that many institutions representative of other models are "headed in this [global] direction" (p. 90).

Hanna (1998) includes several tables that detail differences between models on twelve variables: philosophy, mission, funding, curricula, instruction, faculty, students, library, learning technology, productivity outcomes, governance, and accreditation. However, Hanna also recognizes the models have ambiguous boundaries that will likely continue to blur as organizations opt for combinations of models to best suit their specific, strategic objectives. Although the organizational models may merge, new ones may also appear over time.

Two New Institutional Taxonomies

The same confusion and need to develop new definitions for emerging higher education forms also pushed Wolf and Johnstone (1999) to develop a new institutional taxonomy. The taxonomy would recognize the new forms of communication and education through technology, new combinations of organizations, and new arrangements for organizations. They also developed seven new categories in their taxonomy.

A *virtual university* would not have a campus but would grant academic degrees, much like Western Governors University or the National Technological University.

A *virtual university consortium* would include more than one accredited institution not granting degrees but linked together online. The institutions in the consortium would furnish centralized or coordinated coursework to students, which is in turn articulated among the partners in the consortium.

An *academic services consortium* would include accredited institutions that do not grant degrees but are linked together online and offer centralized or coordinated coursework to students, but without articulation among partners in the consortium.

A *university information consortium* would include accredited institutions, linked together online, but not offer degrees or coordinated services to students.

A *virtual program* would grant degrees (without a student coming to campus) by a traditional accredited institution where the majority of services are offered face-to-face.

A *virtual certification institution* would grant certificates but not award academic credit.

The *traditional accredited institution with electronic courses* would award credit but not offer a coherent program of study leading to a degree.

These distinctions recognize several innovations in the development of higher education: use of online courses and student services, and also collaborative models or consortia. In addition, this taxonomy recognizes that perhaps some institutions will follow a rough developmental arc from being a traditional accredited institution with electronic courses to a virtual program, to membership in one of the consortial arrangements. Such a development is not guaranteed but probable, given commitment to offering education and services online.

Carchidi (2002) also attempted a typology that differentiated organizational types on two axes: delivery of educational services or product and organizational structure. Delivery of educational services or product ranged from place-bound services or products to place-variable or distributed services or products. Organizational structure ranged from centralized to decentralized (also from stable to dynamic organization). This framework resulted in six institutional types:

1. *Insular institution:* this institution is centralized, traditional, and place-bound.
2. *Extended institution:* by redesigning instructional delivery and services, institution is no longer place-bound.
3. *Stable network organization with place-bound offerings:* this institution uses partner arrangements to deliver co-located face-to-face or place-bound courses.
4. *Stable network organization with remote offerings:* this institution uses stable outsourcing arrangements to deliver technology-mediated courses.
5. *Virtual organization with place-bound offerings:* this organization is more likely to appear in corporate settings where training is offered onsite.
6. *Virtual institution:* this institution uses technology to deliver services and products to various places using decentralized approaches (Carchidi, 2002, pp. 7–8).

Four Models of Virtual Universities

From their review of then-current virtual organizations in public higher education, Epper and Garn (2003) also discussed the evolution of four models for the virtual university. As noted in Chapter One, Epper and Garn (2003) found that four models had emerged: the distributed agency model, central agency model, distributed enterprise model, and central enterprise model. By 2003, the existing VUs were falling into two main—and distinctly different—models: centralized and decentralized. Centralized models offered services by a single or central body; decentralized models had participating institutions offer their own services to support faculty and students.

These typologies and new definitions help us better understand the phenomenon of virtual universities, their various permutations, their difficult-to-categorize organizations. This quick review of these classification schema, although complicated, will help us avoid three mistakes. First, just because any two organizations are called "virtual universities," they can still differ in funding, governance, and policy structures. Using one label implies more similarity among VUs than is the case. Second, some forms of the VU are clearly not so different from the traditional higher education institution. In this case, the label implies more difference between traditional and virtual universities than is always the case. Third, many VUs were not separate or for-profit entities, although perhaps the early model (Western Governors University) was such a body. In other words, it is important not to judge all virtual institutions by one example. In fact, there is much more variability than one might expect.

References

Carchidi, D. M. *The Virtual Delivery and Virtual Organization of Postsecondary Education.* New York: Routledge Falmer, 2002.

Epper, R. M., and Garn, M. *Virtual College and University Consortia: A National Study.* Boulder, Colo.: State Higher Education Executive Officers, 2003.

Hanna, D. E. "Higher Education in an Era of Digital Competition: Emerging Organizational Models." *Journal of Asynchronous Learning Networks,* 1998, 2(1), 66–95.

Wolf, D. B., and Johnstone, S. M. "Cleaning up the Language: Establishing a Consistent Vocabulary for Electronically Delivered Academic Programs." *Change, 31*(4), July/August 1999, 34–39.

KATRINA A. MEYER is associate professor of higher and adult education at the University of Memphis.

NEW DIRECTIONS FOR HIGHER EDUCATION • DOI: 10.1002/he

3

Operating principles and policies that have proven successful in the development and operation of WashingtonOnline, a virtual consortium of the thirty-four community and technical colleges in Washington State.

Lessons Learned from WashingtonOnline

Connie Broughton

People do not want to know the history, minutiae of policy, or operations, or even the political intrigues of a virtual consortium. People want to know if the consortium has value, whether it can help them, and if it is a threat. This article focuses less on the operational details of WashingtonOnline (http://www.waol.org) and more on larger lessons from eleven years of operation:

1. Build centralized business processes, take advantage of existing decentralized instruction and support services, and outsource technical services.
2. Create equality of opportunity for all colleges in the consortium.
3. Always ask, "What is best for the students?"
4. Put a high value on faculty professional development.
5. Do not overcommunicate the details, and do not undercommunicate the value.

Background and History

WashingtonOnline (WAOL), a consortium of the thirty-four community and technical colleges in the state of Washington, was funded by the system colleges in August 1997 with the mission to increase access for the citizens of Washington State. Given nineteen months and $530,000, WashingtonOnline was asked to develop twenty completely online courses that would constitute an associate of arts degree, and to build a system to pool enrollments so member colleges could share the courses. The first six courses were offered fall 1998, and the program grew rapidly.

New Directions for Higher Education, no. 146, Summer 2009 © Wiley Periodicals, Inc.
Published online in Wiley InterScience (www.interscience.wiley.com) • DOI: 10.1002/he.342

In all, WAOL has funded colleges to develop ninety-two completely online courses that any college can offer as a shared course with pooled enrollments through WAOL, offer solely to its own students using WAOL, or offer to its own students through the college's course delivery system. In addition, using their own resources, colleges have developed almost three hundred completely online courses that they are willing to share with other colleges using WAOL pooled enrollment functions.

WAOL is charged to create efficiencies both in course delivery and in operations. In its first year of operation, WAOL supported just over 300 annualized FTE with a staff of three. Funded by a FIPSE Learning Anytime Anywhere grant from 2001 through 2005, WAOL staff grew to 9.5 FTE, and by 2002 enrollments nearly tripled to 877 annualized FTE (see Table 1). Benefiting from automation of processes and a mature Website for students and faculty, WAOL supported more than 5,000 annualized FTE for colleges in the 2007–08 year with a staff of eight. In 2008–09, a staff of seven expects to support an additional 20 percent growth and serve 6,000 annualized FTE.

WAOL staffing levels are deceptive because they do not take into account the effort of administrators, staff, and faculty at individual colleges. In addition, the WAOL staff in the early 2000s built the automated programming that allows continued growth today. However, this model has permitted increasing enrollment without growing WAOL staff and fulfills the principles upon which WAOL operates: (1) high growth, scalability (to larger and larger enrollments), and quality realized through centralized, outsourced hosting; (2) tight business rules to achieve maximum automation and integration; (3) technical support twenty-four hours a day, seven days a week, including a high-touch support office; (4) required faculty training; and (5) a dedicated staff with a clear mission and administrative support.

WAOL has always outsourced the course management system (CMS) and round-the-clock technical support services. WAOL will continue to "buy" rather than "build" whenever possible so that staff and colleges can focus on teaching and learning rather than on the technology that can be supplied more cheaply and reliably from technology companies.

Currently, WAOL offers pooling so colleges can share enrollments in a simple automated process; shared development of online courses and

Table 1. Comparison of Annualized Student FTE Supported by WAOL and WAOL Staff FTE

Year	Annualized Student FTE	Staff FTE
2001	877	9.5
2008	5,000	8
2009	6,000 (est.)	7

NEW DIRECTIONS FOR HIGHER EDUCATION • DOI: 10.1002/he

programs; course delivery, including round-the-clock technical support for faculty and students; free online training for faculty and student services staff; a searchable catalog and other information on the WAOL Website, where colleges can advertise their online courses and programs at no cost; and free, unlimited access to Web conferencing through a systemwide license with Elluminate.

How WAOL Works

WAOL is classified as a central business model by Epper and Garn (2004). As such, WAOL relies on centralized business services and decentralized instruction and support services. In most cases, the services already exist at the colleges, and when colleges can offer those services online all students at the college benefit, not just those students who are learning in online courses. By having colleges develop courses that are already offered face-to-face, by enrolling students through existing college processes, and by using existing college accreditation and existing faculty, WAOL built an online support structure that colleges could use to expand the courses, programs, and services they were already offering to their students.

Member colleges have been clear that they do not want a separate entity that enrolls students; they want a virtual organization that supports colleges. Students enroll at the college of their choice, and student enrollments from any participating college can be pooled into shared courses. When colleges choose to adopt shared courses as their own, support services, transcripts, financial aid, and degree completion are seamless for the student. The college that enrolls the student collects all state funds as well as tuition and fees and then pays an instruction fee to the college that hired the instructor. The enrolling college also pays a per-credit technology fee to support WAOL. Colleges hire, supervise, and pay faculty, using the processes already in place at each college.

As the demand for online courses grew, colleges saw that they could fill online classrooms with their own students alone, so WAOL began to support courses where instructors and students are all at the same college. For these courses, WAOL is a hosting service that is well integrated into the technology and operations of the colleges. Because all thirty-four colleges share the same legacy student management system, WAOL programming allows a college to identify courses it wants WAOL to support by inserting a WAOL ID number in the class record. Once students enroll, their information is pulled into the WAOL database, courses duplicated each quarter, and students given access. The WAOL database manages the course capacity, using a cascading enrollment system, so the first section fills first, then the second section, and so on. For shared courses, instructors use a Web grading tool to push grades back to the enrolling college.

NEW DIRECTIONS FOR HIGHER EDUCATION • DOI: 10.1002/he

All Boats Float

In addition to this basic management, WAOL has developed reports and tools that make it easy for colleges to use WAOL and benefit from collaboration: pass-through billing, common faculty training modules developed by WAOL and colleges, a searchable listing of online courses and programs, translation tables that show students how courses transfer from college to college, and a calendar tool that allows the college to choose the start and stop dates. These tools allow a smaller college, or one just beginning an online program, to manage online courses without its own internal programmers or without buying and managing a CMS.

As an incubator for online courses and programs, WAOL provides each college—no matter its size or location—with turnkey access to complete courses, hosted services, faculty training, and student support resources. Some larger colleges do not use WAOL and have developed strong online programs alone; however, smaller colleges do not have the same resources. Over eleven years, all thirty-four colleges have used WashingtonOnline in some way. At the end of 2008, thirteen colleges were relying on WAOL completely to support their online courses, six colleges were not using WAOL for online courses, and the remainder used WAOL for some shared courses and delivering other courses.

According to data from the Washington State Board for Community and Technical Colleges, between 1999 and 2007 online learning in Washington community and technical colleges grew 715 percent. Currently, twenty-three of the thirty-four colleges offer a total of eighty-six degrees and certificates completely online, and sixteen colleges offer a completely online AA degree. These numbers do not include extensive use of hybrid and Web-enhanced classrooms (Washington State Board for Community and Technical Colleges, n.d., b).

In 2007–08, WashingtonOnline supported more than 25 percent of online activity in the system. Although enrollments through WAOL continue to grow at around 30 percent per year, enrollments in shared courses are flat. Consequently, WAOL has focused development dollars on college-initiated projects such as an online tool to track clinical experiences, information literacy modules that can be adapted by individual colleges, and a pool of math assessments.

Shared Course Development. The more businesslike the function, the easier it has been for colleges to adopt. For example, colleges have found it easy to adopt consortium tools or processes because they are simple to use and cost-efficient. However, colleges have found it much harder to adopt courses, instructors, or curriculum, sometimes because the curriculum is not a good fit but often because sharing curriculum and instructors is not the custom in our colleges.

The original twenty courses were general educational requirements for an associate of arts (AA) degree, and these are still the most successfully

NEW DIRECTIONS FOR HIGHER EDUCATION • DOI: 10.1002/he

shared courses. Other attempts to develop complete online programs that can be shared have not been as successful. Because the general education credits of the AA degree must be designed to transfer to a four-year school, they are taught very much the same at every college. The technical and professional programs, however, divide similar course content very differently. Colleges are interested in pooling enrollments in less common courses, but these courses cannot be shared in the same wholesale way colleges share transfer courses. These new collaborations for courses and programs will require close partnerships and are likely to be on a smaller scale.

Cost Model. After the initial grant, each college contributed $6,500 annually to fund the consortium. Because of these funds, WAOL staff do not have to distinguish among colleges for permission to use WAOL services, but at the same time colleges can choose which services to use, when, and how much. In time, a pass-through technology fee became another source of income for WAOL. This per-credit per-enrollment technology fee works well for small users of WAOL, but as a college grows its online program it can cost a college more to use WAOL than to support its own CMS.

As online course delivery became common, colleges that originally relied on WAOL began to move to their own CMS. At the same time, enrollments in shared courses flattened as colleges found they could fill their own sections of courses and did not need to use the pooled sections. Although the value of WAOL to smaller colleges in the community and technical college system is clear, it has become possible for WAOL to work itself out of existence, and the growing online programs at individual colleges might overcome the value of a virtual consortium.

System Technology Plan. WAOL is now at the center of a new system technology plan that addresses some of these challenges and moves the operation to the next level. Starting in 2009, WAOL will add new tools to existing services and will use a new cost model that is more affordable than what a college can do alone. Shared content will be available to colleges not only as complete courses but also in a searchable content repository that uses open educational resources and thereby reduces the need for textbooks in most common courses. In 2008–09, WAOL will move from Blackboard to ANGEL and to a new delivery model whereby colleges can operate from their own domain with their own branding and administrative access. With these changes, some colleges that currently operate their own course delivery system will move back to WAOL.

Focus on Student Learning

When people focus on what is best for students, the answers are clear: "Two-thirds of the 2,033 representative survey respondents—all interested in online education over the next several years—preferred to enroll in online programs located in their state, but only 47 percent had done so; the rest were enrolled in institutions located elsewhere" (Guess, 2007, p. 3).

NEW DIRECTIONS FOR HIGHER EDUCATION • DOI: 10.1002/he

Data from the Washington State Board for Community and Technical Colleges confirm this research. Even when offered opportunities to enroll in online courses from colleges all over the state, most students enroll in the college closest to where they live; therefore opportunities, tools, and products should be available to all colleges regardless of size and location (Washington State Board for Community and Technical Colleges, n.d., a).

Courses and resources should also be offered to all kinds of students. Ten years ago, the WAOL Website stated that online courses are only for students who have strong reading, writing, and study skills. Although strong students continue to do well in online courses, WAOL and system colleges have since developed precollege developmental, adult basic education, and ESL online materials and courses, including adult basic education math modules developed around specific job training skills. Students are successful in all these courses.

Pooled enrollments that allow a college to expand its course offerings have a high value to students, and the college only pays for the students who enroll in the course. However, colleges find it hard to adopt courses developed at other colleges. Instructors fear that an online course will take students away from face-to-face classes, and they question the quality of courses developed at other colleges. However, if colleges do not offer enough seats in online classes or full online programs, students who have the resources will go elsewhere.

One program served by WAOL is a case in point. The Reservation-Based Program is a partnership between the community and technical colleges and Evergreen State College, a four-year college in Olympia, Washington. Students who live on Native American reservations in western Washington can enroll through one of Washington's community colleges (Grays Harbor College) into a special AA degree program. The courses for this program come from sixteen other community and technical colleges, chosen for relevance and excellence and taught by faculty paid to redevelop their online courses to be culturally welcoming. The students complete an AA degree primarily online, but they also meet several times each quarter on the Evergreen campus with upper-division students. Grays Harbor developed wrap-around student services to serve the students, including a dedicated staff person to recruit, enroll, and help with financial aid. Students meet weekly face-to-face with study leaders who help them keep on track and assist with technical issues. This hybrid model has been very successful, is cost-effective, and is scalable to serve more students.

A small rural college would be challenged to support a program like this, and with Native Americans, as is true of other populations in small communities or small populations in large communities, the cultural advantage of learning with peers is difficult to supply. This model can also be replicated for technical programs, serving small numbers of any kind of students who are widely dispersed. Many students cannot be served in every way they need by the local college, but combined together across the entire

New Directions for Higher Education • DOI: 10.1002/he

state they form a critical mass of students. Colleges can then collaborate to serve them efficiently and effectively.

Faculty and Staff Professional Development

WAOL puts a high value on professional development, offering free online courses for student services staff and a required course for all WAOL instructors. WAOL has trained more than two thousand instructors through this completely online course and sees training and support as both student and management issues. The more staff and faculty know about online delivery, the better served students will be. Required training also helps a small WAOL staff support a large number of faculty.

The faculty training class has three outcomes. First, it gives instructors the experience of learning completely online, as their students will. Second, it presents pedagogy of online learning to help instructors translate good face-to-face classes into good online classes. WAOL promotes a highly interactive model for online courses, with heavy reliance on discussion board and group work so that students interact not only with their instructor but also with each other. Third, the class offers training in the CMS.

Ten years ago, few instructors had experience in online teaching or learning. Now many more instructors have online experience, and system colleges have developed more professional development opportunities.

Over- and Undercommunication

One lesson learned after eleven years with a centralized system such as WAOL is that people do not want to know how the machinery works; they want to know how and where they can plug into it. People are not looking for the history; they are looking for the value. The value must be simply expressed: increased access, higher level of interaction, improved technology literacy for the workforce, and better retention.

It has been easier to convince those outside the system of the value of WAOL than insiders. The legislature loves the idea of sharing courses across colleges, but the people who have to get the courses past a curriculum committee, or figure out how money should flow, or deal with a student complaint when the instructor works for another college, sometimes find the simple message difficult to appreciate. If a collaborative business model is imposed on colleges that operate competitively, simple messages are overwhelmed by messy and even confusing details of operation.

Hai-Jew (2004, p. 1) wrote:

> WAOL bears many of the features of a loosely coupled organization with its geographically dispersed frontline instructors, fragmented external environment, modularity of courses and supervision, and its use of enhanced leadership and technology to communicate a culture. . . . Research suggests that

WAOL benefits from some aspects of loose coupling: greater adaptive abilities and responsiveness to the State's college system; "fast" course development and launching; and isolated breakdowns. There is, however, a persistent difficulty in conveying a cohesive culture.

Continuous communication of the value of collaboration is the key to creating a collaborative culture. WAOL's authority comes not from any mandate but from the belief that sharing resources and building a solid delivery system will allow colleges to do more for students.

Although the operational details must be revised, communicated, posted, and explained, the lesson learned is to refine and expand automated processes, outsourced services, and business rules until they become invisible. Then the efforts of WAOL and the member colleges can be directed to what creates true value: improving teaching and learning, supporting faculty and students, and creating more opportunities for learning.

References

Epper, R. M., and Garn, M. "Virtual Universities: Real Possibilities." *EDUCAUSE Review,* 2004, *39*(2), 23–39. http://www.educause.edu/ir/library/pdf/erm0422.pdf.

Guess, A. "Geography Emerges in Distance Ed." *Inside Higher Ed*, 2007, *5*(2). Retrieved Nov. 28, 2007, from http://insidehighered.com/news/2007/11/28/online.

Hai-Jew, S. "WashingtonOnline Virtual Campus: Infusing Culture in Dispersed Web-Based Higher Education." *International Review of Research in Open and Distance Learning,* 2004, *5*(2). Retrieved Dec. 1, 2008, from http://www.irrodl.org/index.php/irrodl/article/view/187/269.

Washington State Board for Community and Technical Colleges. Distance Learning Reports, n.d., a. Retrieved Dec. 1, 2008, from http://www.sbctc.ctc.edu/college/d_distancelearning.aspx.

Washington State Board for Community and Technical Colleges. Strategic Technology Plan, n.d., b. Retrieved Nov. 30, 2008, from http://www.sbctc.edu/college/dl/Strategic TechnologyPlan-final.pdf.

CONNIE BROUGHTON *is the assistant director of e-learning at the Washington State Board for Community and Technical Colleges. She also serves as the managing director of WashingtonOnline.*

NEW DIRECTIONS FOR HIGHER EDUCATION • DOI: 10.1002/he

The approach to offering general education courses online in the University System of Georgia's eCore program.

4

University System of Georgia's eCore: Virtual General Education

Libby V. Morris, Catherine L. Finnegan

In 1995, the Board of Regents of the University System of Georgia (USG) set forth a vision and guiding principles for developing a world-class learning environment. Two principles dealt specifically with the use of educational technology and coordinated public access. In 1999, the board adopted sixteen guidelines to organize its efforts and empower constituents to "employ technologies to expand the learning environment ensuring access to information and educational experiences independent of time, location, and physical boundaries for all types of students from undergraduate through lifelong learners" (USG, 1999).

Spurred by these principles, a subcommittee of the University System's Council on General Education began exploring the potential for online courses, developing requisite policies, and addressing issues of organization. At the time, the USG comprised thirty-four colleges and universities, each offering face-to-face general education courses based on common student-learning outcomes, which are required for courses to be included in the USG core curriculum (http://www.usg.edu/academics/programs/core_curriculum/outcomes.phtmlsystem-level). The subcommittee observed that lower-division courses delivered asynchronously and entirely online by faculty from across the system could include the common student-learning outcomes, meet core curriculum requirements, and offer greater access to students who are nontraditional or at a geographic distance. Thus began eCore, the University System of Georgia's electronically delivered, undergraduate core courses.

NEW DIRECTIONS FOR HIGHER EDUCATION, no. 146, Summer 2009 © Wiley Periodicals, Inc.
Published online in Wiley InterScience (www.interscience.wiley.com) • DOI: 10.1002/he.343

25

This case study reviews the emergence and evolution of eCore over eight years and summarizes the issues, ongoing challenges, and lessons learned from interinstitutional collaboration in offering and administering a "virtual" shared core. The bulk of the literature for online education has focused on issues of teaching and learning online; much less research has focused on the development and administration of online courses and programs (Lasseter, 2008). This case study is informed by our previous research into online education and by eight interviews with administrators at participating "affiliate institutions" and the primary administrative units. Those interviewed held significant positions with the eCore program, and many had been involved since its inception. Of primary interest is the evolution of the virtual core, the management of the collaborative, and issues and challenges that arose from distributed responsibility and accountability.

Emergence of eCore

A primary goal of the eCore subcommittee was to furnish high-quality undergraduate courses in an accessible, interactive, collaborative online environment (http://www.alt.usg.edu/eCore/). In concept, eCore was planned as a highly collaborative integration of university system office capabilities and institutional resources. Two initial planning functions dominated: identifying institutional partners and developing the online courses. eCore is a joint collaborative; it is not a joint program. There are no degrees or certificates, and courses are stand-alone offerings.

Institutional Partners. University system institutions were invited to participate in eCore in three ways: (1) supply faculty to work on cross-institutional course development teams; (2) encourage faculty to teach eCore courses; and (3) admit and enroll students in eCore courses, thereby being named an affiliate institution. Institutions interested in affiliation were asked to furnish a letter of commitment from the institution's president and chief academic officer. Criteria for affiliate selection were (1) diversity by sector, (2) demonstrated commitment to instructional technology, and (3) a statement of institutional interest in and need for the electronic core. Five institutions were initially identified as partners. Two of them—Clayton State University (four-year institution) and Georgia Highlands College (two-year institution)—had established institution-wide laptop initiatives to enhance pedagogy and communication across disciplines. Three other affiliates— University of West Georgia (four-year), Valdosta State University (four-year), and Columbus State University (four-year)—sponsored thriving distance education programs with academic support structures including advising, tutoring, and online services for registration and tuition payment. Soon afterward, Southern Polytechnic State University (four-year) became an affiliate for the primary purpose of offering students enrolled in their online bachelor of information technology degree easy access to the core curriculum.

NEW DIRECTIONS FOR HIGHER EDUCATION • DOI: 10.1002/he

Georgia Southwestern State University (four-year) joined to expand access to its students and others in rural western Georgia.

Affiliates would admit and enroll students, maintain student records, award financial aid, and offer services to distance students, as appropriate, beyond those available centrally. The number of affiliates was intentionally kept small because of the expected modifications that would result from implementation of a Web portal linked with each institution's student information system. Additionally, a smaller group seemed wise given the logistics and business practice modifications expected to accompany the implementation of this new way of offering courses.

The motivations to participate in eCore were varied, and affiliate institutions perceived multiple benefits from the collaboration. First, institutions could increase credit-hour production overall (credit hours followed students). Second, eCore could serve as a marketing tool; that is, eCore students might subsequently matriculate as residential students in traditional courses, thus growing the student population overall. Third, eCore offered elasticity in the core; affiliates were granted additional seats, which could be used by any student, including residential students; consequently, some institutions used eCore as a mechanism to open seats to residential students in heavy enrollment courses, thereby avoiding hiring additional faculty for face-to-face sessions. Finally, eCore was viewed as financially advantageous because affiliates were allowed to charge higher e-tuition rates for eCore courses. In essence, affiliates first embraced the university system goals of access, yet subsequently institutions adapted eCore to meet more pressing institutional priorities, among them advising residential students to take online courses. Institutional participation afforded systemwide visibility and access to system resources for development of online courses. Using Oliver's typology (1990), one sees that institutions' motivation to participate came from reciprocity (through access to resources and efficiency), improving inputs and outputs of student enrollment and offerings, and legitimacy (through improving one's reputation in the system).

Simultaneously with development of eCore, the USG Office of Academics and Fiscal Affairs launched Georgia GLOBE (Global Learning Online for Business and Education). Georgia GLOBE intended to become a highly visible packaging and marketing arm for the system's online presence and was to develop both a full-service informational Website where students could learn about USG online courses and programs and a full-service Web portal where students could exchange information and make financial transactions to enroll in courses and programs. The development of the eCore program proceeded with expectations of substantial support by GLOBE.

Course Development. As partners emerged, course development proceeded. Advanced Learning Technologies (ALT), a unit of the Board of Regents' Office of Information and Instructional Technology, was charged with development of online courses on the basis of recommendations of the eCore subcommittee. ALT professional staff possessed technology expertise, but they did not possess content knowledge; so they formed and coordinated course development teams comprising USG faculty, instructional and online design experts, and technology and multimedia consultants. Early in the evolution of eCore, the Georgia Center for Continuing Education (GA Center) at the University of Georgia played an active role; the GA Center's Web Instructional Development (WebID) Department served on teams and supplied programming and multimedia production services for course development. As eCore moved to implementation, the GA Center role grew even larger.

Ultimately, eighty-three faculty members from thirty USG institutions worked on course development teams of three to six members. The twenty-five semester-long courses were designed to accommodate ten to thirty-five students using a Blackboard platform with multiple faculty members teaching the course over time. Some faculty participated in more than one team. ALT was concerned with quality from the onset, knowing that many faculty viewed online learning with suspicion if not outright hostility. ALT purposefully built courses on a common template using the best principles for teaching and learning online (http://www.alt.usg.edu/research/best/designstds. phtml). Through this standardization, course design issues could be minimized as a factor in student satisfaction, persistence, and achievement, and students enrolling in multiple courses would experience a common look and feel.

A primary issue with course development was integrating faculty into a collaborative planning environment with shared decision making. All of the faculty were subject-matter experts, but most had never taught online, collaborated on the design of a face-to-face course, or participated in peer-review of lesson plans and learning activities. The instructional designer was central to building collaboration and producing a quality course using a common template. In the end, most teams viewed the process as an extremely useful professional development experience, and courses were regarded as high-quality and comparable to (if not better than) the same face-to-face courses (Morris and Xu, 2007).

Evolution and Expansion of eCore

The first six eCore courses were offered in fall 2000: two in English, two in mathematics, one in American history, and one in political science. ALT led nonstop course development, and by summer 2002 enough courses were available to allow students to complete general education requirements online and satisfy lower-division requirements for most majors across the university system. After the affiliates were in place and as the number of courses continued to climb, the primary challenge and priority became program management and partner collaborations.

Staffing Courses. The need to staff courses and enroll students across affiliates grew dramatically between 2002 and 2004 and continued to climb steadily until 2007 (see Figure 1). As more courses were offered online,

NEW DIRECTIONS FOR HIGHER EDUCATION • DOI: 10.1002/he

Figure 1. Growth in Total Enrollment and Course Sections for eCore Courses, FY2001–FY2008

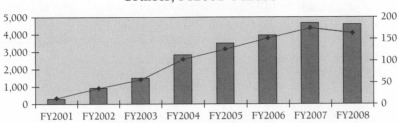

student interest and enrollments increased each term. The increase in courses drove the need for more sections for students, more faculty for teaching, and more need for administrative and academic support services. By spring 2008, a total of 114 faculty from thirty USG institutions had taught one or more eCore courses, and student enrollment stood at nearly five thousand across twenty-five courses and 150 sections.

Enrollment, however, was constrained by a number of factors, and marketing of single courses to an uninitiated and often skeptical public proved nearly impossible. Additionally, "multi-institutional functionality" that allowed multiple student information systems to share course, faculty, and student data had not been considered by major product providers. Georgia GLOBE was ahead of its time and could not deliver. Compounding these problems was a growing demand for faculty experienced in teaching online or interested in doing so.

Program Management. In the emergence phase, ALT was comfortable in the role of course developer and coordinator of enrollments and faculty. But as the complexity of running a virtual, cross-institutional instructional unit grew, ALT needed assistance with evolving academic and administrative roles and sought a partner to assume responsibility for administration of day-to-day operations of eCore. In 2002, ALT negotiated with GA Center, which for nearly forty years had supported credit-bearing correspondence courses and employed faculty to teach students at a distance, to assume some of the administrative functions of eCore.

The ALT–GA Center partnership began with test proctoring services for online students (at least one exam is required to be proctored), and subsequently the GA Center assumed responsibility for hiring faculty, evaluating courses, negotiating with the online bookstore, coordinating registration, distributing grades to appropriate institutions, and adjudicating grade appeals and academic integrity cases. Over time, the GA Center added enrollment counseling, library services, tutoring, and disability services. In effect, the GA Center became a successful "home" to an undergraduate credit-bearing program and acted as a "college" without a dean, department chair, regular faculty, or formalized academic policies by the affiliates.

Reaching Stasis: Challenges and Issues

The GA Center successfully administered eCore through several years of growth and expansion. Yet the distributed nature of the collaborative was not without challenges. Many student issues and faculty issues required ongoing attention.

Student Issues. Enrolling students in courses was an ongoing challenge to institutional affiliates and individual students. From the outset, software to share student enrollments (that is, seats in courses) among affiliate institutions was unavailable, and much of the reassigning of seats, if one of the affiliates did not fill its share, was done manually. Additionally, more e-sections might be up and running than actually were needed, yet moving students around was not possible because of the technology and employment of distributed faculty. Frustration with the absence of a single automated system for handling multiple registrations across multiple campuses was mentioned by almost all of those interviewed. Much to the program's relief, a new system will soon handle this problem.

Because course enrollments took place through affiliate institutions, students not regularly enrolled at an eCore affiliate were required to apply for admission as transient students at a participating institution. These students were often confused as to which affiliate institution to enroll through, whether that decision really mattered, and how to do this. In reality, students had to meet admission standards at the institution of matriculation, and admission standards were not the same for all affiliates. It is not known how many students failed to enroll in eCore because they did not understand this process. Over time, the GA Center employed an advisor to help students through this process. Additionally, some affiliates employed on-campus advisors for eCore. This model was most prevalent at institutions with strong residential enrollment.

Grade Disputes and Withdrawals. Other student issues were more academic in nature, and grade disputes and withdrawals were especially problematic. In the beginning it was not foreseen that collaboration would result in layers of academic policies, and thus the collaborative did not develop a system of academic policies unique to eCore. Instead, the policies of each institution were in play whenever students had an academic dispute or wished to withdraw from a course. For example, a student might be regularly enrolled in a nonaffiliate institution, be a transient in an affiliate institution, and be taught by a faculty member from a third institution. In this case, each party to the collaboration (two individuals and three institutions) might wish or require to apply its institutional policies for a grade dispute. In some cases, eCore faculty did not want to participate in withdrawals because they did not perform that role on their home campus; in other situations, department chairs were brought into "disputes" because they had to sign for students to withdraw on their campus. The complexities are too numerous to enumerate here. As noted by one person, "One of the challenges is to create a unit in a sense, out of these six units."

NEW DIRECTIONS FOR HIGHER EDUCATION • DOI: 10.1002/he

Student Advisement. Institutions also varied in how they supported and "directed" students. One affiliate required students to meet with an advisor before enrolling in an eCore course; others raised retention in courses by dedicated advising and tutoring, and monitoring student enrollment and progress; other affiliates required students to do an "online readiness" tutorial before being admitted to a course. Over time, the affiliate support provided to students became an indicator of greater and lesser degrees of commitment to eCore overall.

The concern over student retention and course completion was a greater issue at the management level than at the institutional level; statistics were reported for courses, not necessarily for institutions. Also, it was important to the program directors (ALT and the GA Center) not to damage the reputation of an emerging program with a low retention rate. Consequently, ALT sponsored several studies to examine the causes of retention and factors for improving student success (Morris, Finnegan, and Wu, 2005; Morris, Wu, and Finnegan, 2005); the findings were widely shared in training sessions with affiliates and instructors.

Faculty Employment. Staffing courses posed an ongoing human resource issue for eCore, and as time passed, the need for a constant pool of faculty mounted. Academic programs in colleges and departments have a core faculty, many of whom are tenured, to offer courses each term, but the GA Center was faced with employing instructors on a course-by-course, semester-by-semester basis. Additionally, administrators were constantly trying to balance course offerings with student demand and instructor availability. These decisions often converged near the beginning of the term, when finding an instructor with previous online teaching experience was critical and the window for training had passed.

The lack of uniform policies also affected faculty performance and turnover. For example, some faculty members were reimbursed separately for eCore while others were assigned the task as part of their regular instructional load. Dissatisfaction with online teaching likely contributed to some turnover; other instructors used eCore to develop online expertise and then used this skill as a competitive edge as they applied for other faculty positions. Although many instructors returned to teach each semester in eCore, any attrition was problematic because locating new instructors posed problems. As shown in other studies of online education (Sixl-Daniell, Williams, and Wong, 2006), finding and training new faculty left administrators scrambling to staff courses just before the term began.

Course and Instructor Evaluations. Course quality and student learning were high priorities for the administration, and the GA Center and ALT used multiple methods to improve instructor performance. One administrator noted that eCore had been a large faculty development effort, employing and training more than two hundred faculty members over eight years, including workshops every semester for all eCore faculty. ALT also offered an instructional designer and faculty developer for real-time, within-course assistance to aid the instructional and technology aspects of the course. Faculty availed themselves of this service to varying degrees.

Student course evaluations were implemented by the GA Center. Student participation never reached the level desired by the administration; nevertheless, workshop modules emerged from student feedback, the online literature, and research completed on student behaviors online in eCore (Finnegan, Morris, and Lee, 2008–09). Unclear lines of authority, however, resulted in difficult situations if instructors were not performing well. It was especially problematic for students if instructors expected the course to "teach itself," because of the highly structured nature of the online course. The GA Center and ALT recognized that novices would not have the same skills as "experts," and instructors would not necessarily be proficient in the online environment even after undergoing training (Morris, Xu, and Finnegan, 2005). The cost of faculty turnover was never calculated, yet attrition in faculty employment has a cost to online programs as well as students (Dooney, 2005; Rodgers, 2002).

Coordinating and Managing Institutional Affiliates. Even though the primary contacts on each campus were in constant communication with each other and with GA Center, GA Center administrators made campus visits every year not only to enact role responsibilities but also to build personal relationships with those involved with eCore. As the literature on collaboration asserts (Lasseter, 2008), much of the success of eCore (growth, sustainability) was attributed to the personal relationships among individuals in the affiliates who were committed to eCore and wanted it to work for students.

The affiliates noted that the lack of a marketing plan for eCore was likely both a structural and political issue (Bolman and Deal, 2003). Over time, participation by the affiliates strengthened for some and weakened for others, leading to discussion of how to solve the lingering student and faculty problems associated with distribution and collaboration.

The Future and Transformation

Overall, eCore is a success: student demand remains strong, courses are regularly updated and evaluated, and interest in online offerings continues to grow. Additionally, several important byproducts and outcomes were associated with development of eCore: dozens of faculty developed expertise in teaching online, many asynchronous courses emerged across the system, and the system supported a limited number of online degree programs, such as the master's in information technology. ALT placed learning objectives developed for eCore into a learning object repository as resources for faculty and other courses. Most recently, ALT launched a request for proposals (RFP) for "virtual franchises" whereby institutions could compete for financial resources to develop online degree programs. Afterwards, the franchise would hold limited, exclusive rights to these online degrees within the system. The franchise model has a long history in business, but its application in higher education is still evolving. The RFPs created a lot of interest and applications for virtual degrees.

The distributed nature of eCore made it everyone's child, and no one's child. The eCore program represented a "shared resources" collaboration (Schermerhorn, 1979); it was more than an information exchange on virtual courses in the system, and yet it was not actually a joint program, because there was some independence in decision making at the faculty and institutional levels. Still, interdependence had to be negotiated by participants (Donaldson and Kozoll, 1999) and multiple individuals had some responsibility to make courses happen each term.

In the end, eCore was not scalable. It seemed to suffer from the same dilemma as general education: no academic home, taught by faculty with allegiance to their discipline, with little connectivity between courses, and a changing student body. The challenges were many. The initiators of eCore, even though planning for technical challenges of offering online courses, were not prepared for academic and administrative challenges. eCore needed a sustainable business model situated within an academic home for the future. ALT and the GA Center, along with the affiliates, brought eCore to maturity; our interviews indicate that sustaining the model for future growth would challenge the structure. Full implementation was accomplished, but transformation—moving to the next stage—posed problems. Structural issues were multiple and compounded by human resource issues. Political issues, though not mentioned by any institutional participants, were likely diminished by the organizational structure, which purported "equity" between the partners. In reality, however, political considerations drove many decisions, from establishment of institutional participants by sector to construction of curriculum teams.

Despite problems, all of those interviewed said that any quality attributed to eCore resulted from the high caliber of courses and the commitment of administrators and supporters across the system. eCore effectively serves many students in repeated semesters, as noted by one student who gained access to postsecondary education through eCore and is now entering a Ph.D. program. As this case study was coming to a close, the university system office decided to move eCore to the University of West Georgia, one of the most active affiliates. Many lingering problems are likely to be addressed quickly under a single administrative structure, but new challenges await. Most important, under a single institution's administration, can eCore ultimately become an integrated, mainstream, systemwide core?

References

Bolman, L. G., and Deal, T. E. *Reframing Organizations: Artistry, Choice, and Leadership.* San Francisco: Jossey-Bass, 2003.

Donaldson, J. F., and Kozoll, C. E. *Collaborative Program Planning: Principles, Practices, and Strategies.* Malabar, Fla.: Krieger, 1999.

Dooney, J. "Cost of Turnover." *Society of Human Resources Management,* Nov. 2005. Retrieved Apr. 22, 2008, from http://www.shrm.org/login.asp?clickth=http://www.shrm.org/research/briefly_published/ROI%20Series_%20Cost%20of%20Turnover.asp.

Finnegan, C., Morris, L. V., and Lee, K. "Differences by Course Discipline on Student Behavior, Persistence, and Achievement in Online Courses of Undergraduate General Education." *Journal of College Student Retention,* 2008–09, *10*(1), 39–54.

Lasseter, M. R. *Inter-institutional Planning of Online Programs in Higher Education.* Unpublished doctoral dissertation, University of Georgia, Athens, 2008.

Morris, L. V., Finnegan, C., and Wu, S. "Tracking Student Behavior, Persistence, and Achievement in Online Courses." *Internet and Higher Education,* 2005, *8*(3), 221–231.

Morris, L. V., Wu, S., and Finnegan, C. "Predicting Retention in Online General Education Courses." *American Journal of Distance Education,* 2005, *19*(1), 23–26.

Morris, L. V., and Xu, H. "Collaborative Course Development for Online Courses." *Innovative Higher Education,* 2007, *32*(1), 35–48.

Morris, L. V., Xu, H., and Finnegan, C. "Roles of Faculty in Teaching Asynchronous Undergraduate Courses." *Journal of Asynchronous Learning Networks,* 2005, *9*(1), 65–82.

Oliver, C. "Determinants of Interorganizational Relationships: Integration and Future Directions." *Academy of Management Review,* 1990, *15*(2), 241–265.

Rodgers, K. "Lessons in HR Metrics." *Webster Buchanan Research,* 2002. Retrieved Apr. 22, 2008, from http://www.websterb.com/articles.php?ID=8c28386503551212.

Schermerhorn, J. R., Jr. "Interorganizational Development." *Journal of Management,* 1979, *1*, 21–38.

Sixl-Daniell, K., Williams, J. B., and Wong, A. "A Quality Assurance Framework for Recruiting, Training (and Retaining) Virtual Adjunct Faculty." *Online Journal of Distance Learning Administration,* 2006, *9*(1).

University System of Georgia. *Educational Technology and the Age of Learning: Transforming the Enterprise,* 1999. Retrieved Dec. 3, 2008, from the USG Web site: http://alt.usg.edu/publications/transformingtheenterprise.pdf.

LIBBY V. MORRIS is professor of higher education and director of the Institute of Higher Education at the University of Georgia.

CATHERINE L. FINNEGAN is director of assessment and public information, advanced learning technologies, Board of Regents of the University System of Georgia.

NEW DIRECTIONS FOR HIGHER EDUCATION • DOI: 10.1002/he

5

The Western Governors University underwent a change in mission during its early years.

Western Governors University: Creating the First Virtual University

Katrina A. Meyer

Distance education in its many forms had been around for decades, but the Western Governors University (WGU) was arguably the first "virtual university" (VU) in the United States, or at least the first VU that gained widespread attention from the press and public. After the governors in the Western Governors Association announced they would create a western virtual university in 1995, WGU became a popular focus of the media, with 189 stories from 1995 to 2008 in the *Chronicle of Higher Education*. The academic literature also contains many mentions of WGU, as an example of a virtual university (Miller, Martineau, and Clark, 2000), as a model of innovation (Baer, 1998), and as a threat to the status quo (Graves, 1997). Additional reports (Epper and Garn, 2003; McCoy and Sorensen, 2003; Twigg, 2003) track the growth in VUs or the possible changes they might generate. Despite this attention from politicians, journalists, and some in academe, it is intriguing that so little research has focused on WGU as an institution, on its innovations, or its impact on higher education.

Breaking the Mold

In its early years, WGU often broke the mold of what a higher education institution would be. Chief among these distinctions was active leadership by governors. It is true that public higher education is overseen by boards whose members are nominated by governors, but the leadership of governors in WGU was both more active and more direct, taking the form of

NEW DIRECTIONS FOR HIGHER EDUCATION, no. 146, Summer 2009 © Wiley Periodicals, Inc.
Published online in Wiley InterScience (www.interscience.wiley.com) • DOI: 10.1002/he.344

day-to-day direction. WGU would operate in several states, siting early business and academic offices in two states (Colorado and Utah), making use of distance programs from institutions in many states, and recruiting students from any state. It would seek accreditation, and demand that the regional associations work together on designing a process for it to follow. It would not offer any courses of its own; therefore it would not need to hire faculty. And it would certify learning through an assessment process that both guided the student through coursework and also split the process of earning credit from the granting of a certificate or degree.

Kinser (2002) studied the early development of WGU, attending planning meetings, reviewing planning documents, and interviewing early leaders. In Kinser's view, three important implications can be gleaned from WGU's emphasis on competency-based distance education. WGU affected the regional accreditation associations by pressuring them to develop a common set of guidelines for distance education (Council of Regional Accrediting Associations, 2001). WGU also implemented a plan to disaggregate the faculty role by having individuals perform different roles (such as teaching, assessment, advisement) traditionally performed by one individual. Finally, "the governors did more than simply create a new university. They created a new organizational pattern for the provision of postsecondary education" (Kinser, 2002, p. 168). Even so, the organizational model for higher education presented by WGU has not been the topic of further research.

Changes and Redirections

To focus on changes within WGU, Meyer (2005) used qualitative methodology to study the question, What critical decisions shaped the development of WGU? Lippitt's model of organizational change (1972) guided the development of the interview protocol, which focused on variables important to organizations as they contemplate, implement, and understand organizational change.

Interviews were held in 2003 with several key informants involved in the creation and current operation of WGU. Individuals who agreed to be interviewed included WGU's earliest staffperson responsible for its design and formation and a then-current staffperson (in the material that follows, these individuals are designated Staff A and Staff B). Representatives from other organizations that consulted with WGU during its early stages were also interviewed, among them individuals from the Western Cooperative for Educational Telecommunications and the State Higher Education Executive Officers organization (these individuals are designated Consultants A, B, and C). The author was also involved in the early stages of WGU and served for several years on two committees: the States Advisory Committee and Academic Affairs Committee. However, the author's perceptions were evaluated by interviewees.

New Directions for Higher Education • DOI: 10.1002/he

Each interview discussed seven aspects of organizations and their development: goals, norms or values, persons in charge, problem solving, power relationships, flow of communication, and important decisions. Then interviewees were asked if anything had changed in the organization; they supplied specific examples of decisions and changes.

Several themes emerged from individual answers, and they were evaluated by other interviewees. Twelve themes emerged and were grouped into five categories: politics, organizational models, changing mission, multiple missions, and experiencing innovation.

Politics. First, WGU was born in and shaped by *political forces*, taking the form of high-level politicians who had political agendas and were making political decisions. In the beginning, WGU was pushed and promoted by Governors Leavitt of Utah and Romer of Colorado. This led to a novel organizational arrangement: WGU would be staffed by one person from each state, each with an equal role in the selling, development, and operation of WGU. The early staff spent a great deal of time visiting with "anyone in the partnering states who thought WGU would impact them (such as regents, trustees, gubernatorial staff, institutions, departments, faculty)" (Staff A). Despite the ability of these political entities to demand consultation, however, it was the two founding governors who had the most power and influence on the organization.

Second, this legacy of political leadership also led to instances of *political intrusion*, which was at times distracting. When the meeting of the seven industrial nations (the G7 Summit) was to be held in Denver, Colorado, on June 20–22, 1997, Governor Romer wanted to take advantage of the world stage to promote WGU. "This event took all of the staff's time and attention" (Staff A) for several weeks, which increased the public's recognition of WGU but required so much time and attention of the small staff that no other activities were accomplished.

"Governors are used to getting their way" (Consultant B) and were often oblivious to how much work it would take to fulfill their demands.

> Governors say something is so and [they think] it will happen without regard to how it will happen, who can do it, or the resources needed for the job. This doesn't work, particularly in higher education where people have their time already committed to other work obligations [Consultant A].

Staff were often "more focused on public relations than operations" (Consultant B). This focus may reflect a governor's need to pursue press opportunities and public recognition of gubernatorial achievements, or it may be attributed to the pursuit of publicity for the sake of enrollments. This captures the mixed blessing of efforts begun by politicians: as individuals who depend on public support to get elected and remain so, there is a greater demand for publicity to ensure public support but less understanding of the work required to create a fully functioning organization.

NEW DIRECTIONS FOR HIGHER EDUCATION • DOI: 10.1002/he

Another example of perhaps inappropriate intrusion was the decision to hire staff without consultation. Consultation is valued in higher education, but it was not a priority among politicians. This illustrates a fundamental tension when the world of politics and higher education overlap; the values and cultures of the two fields may conflict in important ways. Which culture survives or influences more decisions is an important question when organizations combine two arenas.

Organizational Models. In the earliest planning documents, WGU was a twofold entity: one part would be a repository of distance education courses from higher education institutions in the West and the other part a provider of competency-based programs. In other words, it would be a "broker" of other institutions' courses and programs, but also grant its own degrees. As it developed, WGU would decide to drop its brokering function and focus on developing its own programs.

One interviewee noted that the brokering function was *not* in the governors' original vision; the governors were not "committed or interested in the brokering function. . . . It was forced upon them as a political compromise with institutions. A new institution that wasn't going to play with existing institutions was really seen as a threat" (Consultant C). Thus the brokering function was adopted to palliate the existing institutions but may never have been a solid commitment on the part of the governors.

Eventually WGU would become an *independent organization* and not a consortium of existing higher education institutions. This decision distinguishes it from the other major regional consortium, the Southern Regional Electronic Campus. In other words, WGU intended from its earliest days to grant degrees, but not to offer its own courses. In contrast, today WGU offers its own courses and grants degrees. To accomplish this, it charged experts to create a list of competencies for each degree and then used the distance education courses offered by participating institutions by identifying which competencies were contained in each course (in WGU-speak, this was termed "mapping" the course against the competencies established for each WGU degree). An assessment for the competencies would be given to students to determine if they possessed the competencies appropriate for the degree. This plan would be easier to conceptualize than to implement.

The decision to grant its own degrees required seeking and gaining regional accreditation, with the incumbent changes to accrediting practices already noted. In turn, accreditors required clear lines of control and responsibility, which encouraged WGU to adopt an organizational model with an executive board, much like traditional institutions. But accreditation was also sought by the early staff in order to have "academic legitimacy" (Staff A) with its future higher education partners and the public.

Changing Mission. First, the decision to focus on competency-based curricula and testing forced out the original mission to provide a repository of distance learning courses for the institutions in the West.

In the very beginning, they really thought that WGU would be a broker of other institutions' courses, and that is where the great number of students would come from. It was a major decision to not focus on other institutions' courses and to only use courses that relate to WGU degrees [Staff B].

This decision illuminates two additional reasons for diminishing the brokering mission of WGU. First, the assumption that WGU could "use" other institutions' courses was limited by whether excess capacity existed in the courses, which was often limited to only a few "slots." Second, WGU needed enrollments in courses that promoted competencies leading to WGU degrees, which forced it to pursue partners with specific programs. Thus it needed to use limited staff to pursue particular partners with excess capacity in areas needed for WGU degrees rather than develop the brokering portion of WGU. This may account for WGU's change in relationship to other higher education institutions, from a "host" in a brokering relationship to a partner who needed to use its partners' courses.

The second reason for dropping the brokering function from its mission was the necessity to seek *financial support* for WGU. The quandary of how to fund the organization led to several decisions. In its infancy, WGU "never had enough money" (Staff A), and the initial business plan developed by consultants depended on two funding streams for ongoing institutional support: fees charged to students and to institutions. However, students avoided the WGU fee by going directly to the institution to enroll in the course, and institutions found the fees excessive when enrollments did not materialize. The issue of enrollment estimates is an important one and justifies a short digression. Early estimates of large student enrollments were especially misleading (see Meyer, 2003, for further analysis). This meant "it became obvious that the institution had to function, do something—offer degrees—so that it could charge for services" (Consultant A). In other words, the pursuit of a reliable and more substantial revenue stream became important, and competency-based degrees were deemed a better source of revenue than hosting a course-sharing site for the West.

Early development of WGU and its programs was funded by foundations and the federal government, totaling $5–7 million from various sources (Staff A). But eventually the organization decided to seek financial support from commercial partners, including a number of technology firms. Funding from corporations soon reached approximately 50 percent of the organization's support, making WGU "more reliant on the commercial partners" (Consultant A). These partners soon had representatives on an advisory board, and the emphasis on competency-based programs triumphed because "the Silicon Valley folks understood and thought it was a great idea" (Consultant A). It is impossible to unravel whether the involvement of corporate partners (and their financial support) preceded or determined the change in focus. In any case, several financial explanations exist for eliminating the brokering function.

NEW DIRECTIONS FOR HIGHER EDUCATION • DOI: 10.1002/he

Multiple Missions. First, the governors crucial to the formation of WGU had *multiple objectives* for the fledgling organization. Leavitt wanted to increase the use of technology to deliver education and address the pressure for additional access across the West. Romer wanted to promote competency-based education. Perhaps one can better grasp the complexity of the role and mission of WGU by reviewing the list of aims included in early vision documents: to increase access to higher education through sharing distance education resources across the Western states (Consultant C), "to make a wider variety of programs available" (Consultant A), "to push higher education to be more responsive to state workforce needs" (Consultant A), to create online student services (Staff B), to revise regional accreditation practices, to "increase the quality of higher education by imposing real outcomes, real quality measures" (Consultant A), to "push assessment of learning and less focus on clock hours" or "seat time" (Staff A). In other words, the governors wanted to use WGU to "drive change through the more traditional institutions in their states" (Staff A). Clearly, a thorough evaluation of WGU's ability to fulfill its various early missions and its legitimate achievements is needed. Especially in the case of WGU's purported goal to "drive change" through traditional institutions, an assessment of WGU's influence is essential.

Second, when WGU abandoned its dual mission to focus on competency-based programs of its own, it had a significant impact on WGU's *role in the West*. "One of WGU's most important decisions was to abandon the clearinghouse goal and to narrowly focus its offerings. This was probably a necessary step, but it left the other states . . . feeling that they had been abandoned" (Consultant B). Many states and institutions then pursued their own statewide or systemwide e-learning catalogs or one-stop sites for locating information about distance learning that was uncoordinated (and unshared) across the West. This trend was borne out by the research done by Epper and Garn (2003).

In other words, it was likely a wise decision for WGU to focus its meager staff and financial resources on one major activity that would make it special and unique among higher education providers. But it may have contributed to a proliferation of e-learning efforts that would be duplicated across the West and discourage the type of sharing of resources originally envisioned for WGU.

Still, it is important to note that in several ways WGU has evolved differently—with a *new mission*—than originally planned. WGU now offers its own courses and programs.

> Most institutions can't support large numbers of new WGU students . . . having WGU students enrolled in a few excess spaces in partners' courses was not scaleable. To handle more students, the growth needed by WGU outpaced the capacity of its partners [Staff B].

Two interviewees called the current WGU a "niche market" institution, having found its role as a unique education provider that offers different programs to students than its competitors across the West. In other words, even though both WGU and traditional institutions may offer the same degree title, WGU offers a competency-based program, distance-delivered and with external assessments.

Experiencing Innovation. This last category does not deal with WGU as an organization, but as an experience for individuals caught up in its formation and development. Every interviewee involved in WGU's creation spoke *enthusiastically* about the experience of trying to create a new type of higher education organization that would be more responsive to students. In other words, the experience was stimulating and challenging. Second, every person also spoke about the *difficulties* faced in creating a new organization, in terms of the amount of time it took, "travel that was wearing on self and family" (Staff A), worries about a failure of imagination or knowledge, and doubt about the organization's future. One consultant stated, "I don't want to repeat the experience, it was one of the 'wildest rides of my life' . . . but if they [the governors] called again, I'd get much more definition on what they want, timeframe, money, who will accomplish, etc." (Consultant A). The staff suffered from having "too many irons in the fire" (Staff A) as they worked on a business plan, curricula, policies, and staffing—which was sufficient work to keep three times the staff busy (Staff A).

It is clear that WGU faced serious problems in its early development, tried to be many things to many people, and was thus saddled with trying to design and implement "too many new inventions" (Consultant B) that were, by definition, untried and untested. Its modest success, which even its critics grant it, would be a triumph of creativity under duress. Under such circumstances, some activities or aims should have been expected to fail. In other words, WGU needed to "promise less, deliver more" (Consultant A) to be successful. No matter how sound in the managerial sense, this was probably not an option acceptable to its political founders.

Another important point to take from the story of WGU was the role that unintended consequences played in its development. For every choice, the consequences were not always clear at the time the decision was made. The choice of WGU to focus on competency-based programs may have meant the end of its brokering mission, but it also meant that each state would eventually create its own brokering efforts.

But these are criticisms advantaged by hindsight. In other words, creating something new and real out of concepts and guesswork is fraught with all kinds of problems and heightens the likelihood that mistakes will be made as well as successes. This should not be surprising. As one interviewee put it, WGU is "an interesting case study of moving from an idea to reality, [from] theory to reality" (Consultant A). Obviously, WGU was, and

NEW DIRECTIONS FOR HIGHER EDUCATION • DOI: 10.1002/he

still is, an appropriate subject for further study about the building of a new higher education organization.

WGU Today

Over a decade after its founding by governors, WGU now offers forty-five programs (twenty-five baccalaureate and twenty master's programs) within four colleges: Teacher's College and colleges of business, information technology, and nursing. Students are drawn from the fifty states, and more than four hundred students graduate from WGU each year. Highlights from a number of surveys and assessments (WGU, n.d.) indicate that 93 percent of students were satisfied with their experience at WGU and 86 percent were satisfied with the mentoring and support received, 95 percent of employers were satisfied with their WGU graduates, and 79.5 percent of students pass their WGU competency exams.

We can conclude that WGU has found its niche in the higher education marketplace and is successful at fulfilling its competency-based mission with satisfied graduates.

Issues

We still have only a few studies of the organization, processes, or programs developed by WGU. This is a shame; WGU seems to offer an opportunity to understand a number of questions about innovation in higher education, novel funding approaches, and what impact if any WGU may have had on higher education. It is a unique institution deserving of the attention of researchers. It is experimenting with a number of new processes—including competency-based education, assessment of learning, new faculty roles—which should be investigated for their impact on student learning. It has developed different types of relationships with partner institutions, business providers, and states, and these also should be evaluated.

What lessons can be drawn from the research on WGU? We know that innovation in higher education happens, although it is often tough to do, taking a lot from the individuals doing it. It may not take the shape originally promised, and it may evolve from attempting too many missions to successfully addressing a more focused mission. In any case, tracing the way innovations morph is an interesting endeavor, and hopefully more researchers will investigate the short-term and long-term impact of WGU's innovations.

References

Baer, W. S. *Will the Internet Transform Higher Education?* Rand Corporation, #RP-685, 1998. Retrieved Dec. 19, 2007, from http://www.rand.org/pubs/reprints/2005/RP685.pdf.

Council of Regional Accrediting Commissions. *Best Practices for Electronically Offered Degree and Certificate Programs*, 2001. Retrieved Dec. 15, 2008, from http://wcet.info/resources/accreditation/Accrediting%20-%20Best% 20Practices.pdf.

Epper, R. M., and Garn, M. *Virtual College and University Consortia: A National Study.* Boulder, Colo.: State Higher Education Executive Officers, 2003.

Graves, W. H. "'Free Trade' in Higher Education: The Meta University." *Journal of Asynchronous Learning Networks,* 1997, *1*(1), 97–108.

Kinser, K. "Taking WGU Seriously: Implications of the Western Governors University." *Innovative Higher Education,* 2002, *26*(2), 161–173.

Lippitt, G. L. *Visualizing Change: Model Building and the Change Process.* Fairfax, Va.: NTL Learning Resources Corporation, 1972.

McCoy, D. R., and Sorensen, C. K. "Policy Perspectives on Selected Virtual Universities in the United States." *Quarterly Review of Distance Education,* 2003, *4,* 89–107.

Meyer, K. A. "The Rule of the Marketplace: How Flawed Beliefs Contributed to the Failure of Dot-coms and Virtual U's." *EDUCAUSE Quarterly,* 2003, *26*(2), 4–7.

Meyer, K. A. "Critical Decisions Affecting the Development of Western Governors University." *Innovative Higher Education,* 2005, *30*(3), 177–194.

Miller, J. W., Martineau, L. P., and Clark, R. D. "Technology Infusion and Higher Education: Changing Teaching and Learning." *Innovative Higher Education,* 2000, *24*(3), 227–241.

Twigg, C. A. *Expanding Access to Learning: The Role of Virtual Universities.* Troy, N.Y.: Center for Academic Transformation, 2003. Retrieved Dec. 20, 2008, from http://www.thencat.org/Monographs/Mono6.pdf.

Western Governors University. "About WGU. Student Success and Performance Data." n.d. Retrieved Dec. 20, 2008, from http://www.wgu.edu/about_WGU/student_success_data.asp.

KATRINA A. MEYER *is associate professor of higher and adult education at the University of Memphis.*

6

How three state-level virtual universities engage colleges and universities in their distance education activities.

A Comparative Case Study of State-Level Virtual Universities

Haixia Xu, Libby V. Morris

The idea for a virtual university was first triggered in the United States by the launch of Western Governors University (WGU) in 1995, and then followed by California, which established the California Virtual University (CVU) in 1997. Although CVU came to a sudden dissolution in 1998, similar initiatives were replicated in other states in the following decade and there came into existence many distance education consortia, or *state-level virtual universities*, although not all bear the name "virtual university." According to the National Center for Educational Statistics (2003), as of spring 2002, 83 percent of public two-year institutions and 68 percent of public four-year institutions participated in distance education consortia of some sort, primarily in the form of state-level virtual universities.

As a recent phenomenon, virtual universities—degree-granting and nondegree-granting consortia alike—were the focus of quite a few articles and reports, yet little information was based on solid data. There is a lack of understanding of what virtual universities do, what value they add, and how complex the collaborative arrangement can be. Of particular interest is how state-level virtual universities work with other higher education institutions in their states in order to achieve their goals.

The purpose of this study was to understand the consortial approach to distance education at the state level, with a focus on examining the way three state-level virtual universities engaged colleges and universities in participating in distance education initiatives. Specifically, three research questions guided this study:

NEW DIRECTIONS FOR HIGHER EDUCATION, no. 146, Summer 2009 © Wiley Periodicals, Inc.
Published online in Wiley InterScience (www.interscience.wiley.com) • DOI: 10.1002/he.345

1. What structure was in place to engage higher education institutions?
2. What services were offered to member institutions?
3. What were the barriers and challenges perceived by member institutions?

Drawing on experiences of participating institutions as well as the management team of the virtual universities, this study examined the interactions between the two groups and demonstrated how the interactions helped to redefine the missions of the organization and influence the strategies used to engage higher education institutions.

Literature Review

A review of the literature suggests that more rigorous research is needed in the field of state-level virtual universities. Many publications have not been based on rigorous research methods, but on opinions and individual case reports. In addition, some of this literature has a narrow focus, limited to understanding the concept of a virtual university (Epper and Garn, 2003; Smith, 1998; Wolf and Johnstone, 1999) or the organizational models of virtual universities (Dutton and Loader, 2002; Farrell, 1999; Hanna, 2000), and creating various frameworks to analyze policies and structures of virtual universities (Berge, 1998; Gellman-Danley and Fetzner, 1998; King and others, 2000; McCoy, 2002; Rosevear, 1999). Researchers have explored the consortial approach to distance education, identifying advantages (such as spreading risk, incorporating new ideas, enhancing competitiveness) and challenges both academic and administrative (Johnson, Hanna, and Olcott, 2003; Kennedy, 2006; Moore, 2003).

Two comprehensive national studies furnished in-depth insight into the roles, policy issues, and challenges of virtual universities in the United States. On the basis of a symposium with thirteen chief executives of virtual universities, Twigg (2003) concluded that virtual universities that rely on an institutional collaborative model may do a good job of supporting institutions as they move to online learning, but it was questionable how effective they were at meeting statewide goals. The Epper and Garn (2003) national survey of sixty-one statewide virtual universities found a shift in goals from broadening access to increasing system higher education efficiency and meeting state workforce needs. Epper and Garn also identified the most common barriers faced by virtual universities as inadequate funding and staffing, lack of collaboration among institutions, fear of competition among institutions, and insufficient understanding of the virtual university by leaders at high levels in institutions and states.

Methodology

This was an in-depth, descriptive case study, using a qualitative approach (Merriam, 1988; Yin, 1994). Three public virtual universities were chosen,

New Directions for Higher Education • DOI: 10.1002/he

each being unique in its own way. Kentucky Virtual University was a pioneer virtual university with a national reputation; Ohio Learning Network excelled in facilitating distance education initiatives by its member institutions, both public and private; UT (University of Texas) TeleCampus distinguished itself by its quality assurance system and its focus on collaborative online degree programs as opposed to individual online courses.

The three virtual universities share some characteristics. First, unlike the stand-alone accredited Western Governors University, they are not "real" universities in the sense of degree granting, but consortia of participating institutions that offer online courses or programs. Second, they were created by the state to reach students who would otherwise have no access to higher education. Accordingly, they were largely funded through legislative action, at least at the start-up stage. Third, they maintain electronic portals containing courses and programs offered online or using other delivery systems, and they offer services to participating institutions (such as technological services, consulting services, grants for developing new programs), to students (such as online registration, online tutoring, help desk), or to faculty (training workshops, grants for delivering new courses).

A total of forty-three people from the three virtual universities participated in this study, primarily representing two groups: the management team of the virtual university and administrators from higher education institutions participating in the virtual university. The administrators were in charge of or directly involved in the distance education initiatives on their campuses, with titles of provost, vice president, dean, and director of distance learning or academic services.

This study relied on two types of data: document analysis and open-ended interviews. A number of relevant documents were collected and reviewed prior to the interviews, including legislation, state reports, and administrative documents, press releases, journal or magazine articles, as well as information retrieved from official Websites. Interviews were conducted in person or by telephone in summer 2005 and spring 2006, and each interview lasted forty-five to ninety minutes.

Research Findings

Kentucky Virtual University. Kentucky Virtual University (KYVU) was created in 1997 as a result of a state higher education reform to (as stated on its official Website) "make Kentucky's postsecondary education system more accessible, efficient, and responsive to Kentucky's citizens and businesses." Its mission was "to be student-centered, technology-based utility for the support of lifelong learning," and its primary goals were to generate "new" students and increase the college-going rate in Kentucky. As one of the earliest state-level virtual universities, KYVU received much national attention as a pioneer in statewide distance education.

New Directions for Higher Education • DOI: 10.1002/he

Kentucky Virtual University started with students as its primary constituency and functioned as a centralized utility provider independent of colleges and universities. According to the interviews, existing higher education institutions resisted the organization. As a result, the majority of enrollments were at two-year colleges, while most of the four-year institutions provided distance education opportunities on their own.

Organizational Structure. KYVU established committees to work with member institutions in guiding its work. The Distance Learning Advisory Committee served as the governing board and was primarily made up of vice presidents and provosts of colleges and universities in Kentucky. Four more committees and workshops served as advisory groups to KYVU. Interviews with member institutions revealed several problems with the structure. For example, most of the people sitting on the committees were campus administrators in charge of distance education, continuing education, or teaching and learning, while "on the ground" folks in the units working directly with distance students (such as the registrar's office) were not included. This omission led to limited support and understanding of KYVU activities and affected the quality of KYVU's daily operation. Another problem was that members on some committees stopped attending meetings; instead, they sent their designees and hence "the same people are sitting in different committee meetings," one interviewee stated. This led to little variability of input into decisions.

Services. When KYVU was launched in 1997, it was designed as a central utility provider independent of colleges and universities in Kentucky, instead of building on existing distance education infrastructure in the state through allocating funds to participating institutions to develop their own services. Consequently, KYVU was considered a competitor, and it became alienated from the higher education institutions.

KYVU invested many resources in the student interface and registration functions, but these services were not positively regarded by colleges and universities. To them, student services were more appropriately the responsibility of institutions. Services that were positively regarded included the digital library, an annual conference on faculty development, and a loan program that helped institutions develop online courses and programs.

Reasons for Lack of Participation. Member institutions offered various reasons for not actively participating in the KYVU activities. First, there was a lack of incentives for large universities to participate. Unlike smaller institutions, larger institutions were not looking for more enrollment. Also, larger institutions had already established self-sufficient distance education services by the time KYVU emerged, which made it difficult for them to participate. Second, there was a lack of identity. Partly because of minimal participation of higher education institutions, shortly after its launch KYVU switched from exclusively serving higher education institutions to serving state agencies and K–12 schools, focusing on workforce development and adult education. This diffused its identity as a higher education entity. Third, it used a top-down approach. A centralized, top-down approach was brought up several times during the interviews. For example, KYVU identified several high-demand courses and requested that colleges and universities offer them online. After repeated rejection, KYVU picked a provider for course development and implementation from outside Kentucky, which enraged the higher education institutions. Fourth, a lack of leadership plagued KYVU. High turnover of leadership partly contributed to the inconsistency of mission and focus.

Ohio Learning Network. The Ohio Learning Network (OLN) was created in 1999 following a statewide committee's recommendation to increase the college-going rate in Ohio. OLN was established to assist colleges and universities by providing educational technologies, faculty development, and statewide shared resources. A consortium of seventy-four member institutions, OLN had a mission (as noted on its Website) "to work in collaboration with higher education, schools, policy makers, business and industry, government, and local communities to expand educational opportunities for Ohioans."

Organizational Structure. OLN worked closely with a large number of higher education institutions, both private and public, through their representatives at various levels. Four committees were established at the founding of OLN, each working with a specific group of administrators or professionals from participating institutions. It is through the various committees that OLN networked with higher education institutions and fostered statewide collaboration among the member institutions.

Services. OLN was not set up to deliver direct services not already provided by institutions. Instead, the primary functions included a Website, grants, an annual conference, and interinstitutional communication and collaboration.

Website: OLN maintained a sophisticated Website that served multiple functions: an electronic catalog, a resource center for faculty and institutions, a tutorial for prospective learners to use to assess their suitability for distance learning, and a communication mechanism for showcasing OLN activities.

Grants: a major OLN activity was providing funding opportunities to postsecondary institutions in Ohio to encourage the development of Web-based content in areas of need as well as to foster collaborative activity in terms of distance learning. Between 1999 and 2008, more than $12 million in grants was awarded to participating institutions to support online education initiatives.

Annual conference: OLN has held an annual conference on online education for faculty and administrators since its inception, with attendees doubling from 150 in 1999 to 385 in 2008.

Interinstitutional communication and collaboration: by sending representatives to OLN committees and developing collaborative online courses and

degree programs, higher education institutions were able to create partnerships with OLN, with peer institutions, and with other state entities.
This networking function was especially helpful to smaller institutions.

Positive Aspects of OLN. Member institutions attributed the success of
OLN to a number of factors. First, *OLN leadership* was effective. The CEO
of the OLN was respected for "balancing out the top-down and bottom-up
approaches very well" while dealing with member institutions. This CEO
was also given much credit for "advocating on behalf of the colleges and
universities at the Board of Regents and the state legislature for our needs."
Second, there was *political and financial support from the state*. Support from
the state was cited as a big enabler. A university administrator who was
involved in OLN since its launching made the observation: "I think the
main one is that the Board of Regents and state legislature have both
expressed the value in distance learning. . . . So when the state thinks it's
valuable, it is willing to put money in it. It's a big factor." Third, *effective
communication* occurred in multiple ways, through committee work, quarterly newsletter, online listserv, and online update. Fourth, OLN used a
decentralized approach. The decentralized approach worked well; as the
CEO explained, "Being a consortium, you can only lead as far as the organizational members are willing to follow. It's a delicate balance. NO dictating. We don't do that. If you are willing to do this, I'll give you the money."
Fifth, *OLN was an advocate*. Several university administrators identified
OLN's function as an advocate for distance learning in the state: "OLN par-
ticipates on behalf of colleges and universities in a political process with the
Board of Regents and the state legislature, something we all can use." Sixth,
OLN services were helpful. The most frequently cited services were grants,
information on the OLN Website regarding teaching and learning at a dis-
tance, and an annual conference on faculty development.

Barriers and Challenges at OLN. Participating institutions identified
several challenges within OLN. Institutions continued to resist collaboration, there was a lack of measurement or a better reporting system, resources
continued to be insufficient to address needs, and there was limited success in
generating "new" students because a large percentage of the students were
already enrolled in traditional courses.

UT TeleCampus. The UT TeleCampus (UTTC) was launched in May
1998 as a result of a six-month study on possible opportunities for collaboration within the University of Texas System using information technology.
The UT TeleCampus was created as a central support unit that facilitated distance education initiatives within the system. UTTC has been nationally recognized for its intercampus collaborative degree programs and for the
expansive array of student services offered in support of distant students.

Organizational Structure. UTTC built a sophisticated network with
member institutions by including people who perform diverse functions at
various levels on campus. According to the CEO:

There are TeleCampus contacts that were appointed directly by presidents on each campus. We communicate regularly. They're our eyes and ears on campuses. . . . We have liaisons in the registrar's office—employed by the campuses—in the admissions office, library, financial aid office. . . . We have people in various departments. . . . I periodically meet with the presidents and provosts when they're in town. We also go to the campuses. Currently in the middle of campus tour right now. We sit down with the presidents and provosts and other people we work with. We also communicate with academic departments regularly. . . . We send out a monthly newsletter that goes to everyone with any interest in the TeleCampus at all, including all the faculty, and officers and deans, providing update on what we do. We have been doing this for three years.

Another unique aspect of the UTTC is its way of working with faculty and academic administrators on quality assurance. For each online program there are two committees: the Academic Affairs Committee, which consists of faculty and conducts peer review of course content; and the Executive Committee, which consists of deans and makes strategic decisions.

Services. UTTC directly assists member institutions in program development and technology services. In addition, it provides services to students and faculty through member institutions. Student services include online tutoring, digital library resources, round-the-clock technical support, and call center; faculty services include technical support; online course and instructor evaluation system; and training opportunities in instructional design, course management, and technology use.

Positive Aspects. Member institutions attributed the success of UTTC to a number of factors. First, both institutional representatives and UTTC staff attributed the organization's achievements to *strong leadership* from the founding CEO at UTTC. A campus liaison expressed high regard for the CEO and her staff: "Much of the TeleCampus's success is due to the persistence and energy of the Director . . . she has also managed to hire effective staff members, who are not only skilled in technology and management, but are good communicators as well." Second, *financial support* from the state was crucial. The CEO at UTTC recognized the UT System's support, especially in the early years of the organization: "We had very strong support from the chancellor at that time . . . and he was willing to provide resources so we were able to build the services. . . . They gave us money and we were able to offer that money to the institutions to help us develop courses." Third, strict *quality assurance* standards were set and followed to ensure quality for online offerings, a step no other virtual university has taken so far. Fourth, *the emphasis on services* largely accounted for the success of the organization. According to an institutional representative, "The UT Tele-Campus services are very good. This is one of the reasons we couldn't build the program all by ourselves. . . . We do not have to build an infrastructure (technological and administrative) to support a full-blown online course

NEW DIRECTIONS FOR HIGHER EDUCATION • DOI: 10.1002/he

service (platform; round-the-clock help, and tutoring service)." Fifth, the organization benefited from *effective communication* with member institutions in multiple forms, such as committee work, campus visits, campus liaisons, and monthly newsletter, which kept member institutions informed of UTTC initiatives and made it possible for UTTC to seek input from the institutions.

Barriers and Challenges Faced by UTTC. Member institutions identified certain challenges. First, the turnover among campus contacts made it necessary to constantly reeducate member institutions about the organization. Second, there was continuing confusion about the criteria for evaluating UTTC performance. Third, sometimes it was difficult working with people on campus thanks to a lack of formal jurisdiction or supervisory relationships. Fourth, institutions continued to resist statewide coordination for fear of an extra layer of control.

Lessons Learned

Lessons learned from establishing and operating a new virtual university may be valuable to those involved in similar initiatives and to those in other higher education settings. The lessons given here will assist state leaders, administrators, faculty members, and others involved in starting a virtual university.

1. Deliberate planning is crucial prior to the establishment of a virtual university. It is important to consult with higher education institutions and seek their input. It is necessary to have a sound strategic plan in place to guide the operation of the virtual university, to stay focused and not become "all things to all people."
2. Make higher education institutions the primary constituency. A virtual university directly serves higher education institutions, not individual learners. Be less of a provider, more of a facilitator. Develop partnerships with existing colleges and universities, and build on existing infrastructures and services. Bring higher education institutions together to share information, solve policy issues regarding distance education, and collaborate on developing or offering online courses and programs. Be cautious about working directly with students or learners; this will only invite resistance and resentment from higher education institutions if a virtual university acts independently of higher education institutions.
3. Secure support and funding from the state. To do so, a virtual university has to demonstrate the value that it adds to the state and to higher education institutions, whether it is increasing enrollments or developing new programs or services. Constantly conduct formal and informal evaluations to measure organizational performance.

NEW DIRECTIONS FOR HIGHER EDUCATION • DOI: 10.1002/he

4. Identify needs of the primary constituencies and provide services in multiple forms for students, faculty, and higher education institutions. Basic services such as course catalog, technical support, call center, and infrastructure (such as a course management system) were generally considered crucial. Grants, annual conferences, and online resources were most valued by higher education institutions. In delivering services, the goal should be to build institutional capacity, not to compete with higher education institutions. It could be dangerous to bypass colleges and universities by providing services directly to students and faculty.

5. Communication is the key. Create committees with various groups of campus participants in terms of level and expertise, including grassroots professionals on campus. Reach out to all the constituencies in multiple ways, and seek feedback from higher education institutions. Lead; do not dictate.

References

Berge, Z. L. "Barriers to Online Teaching in Postsecondary Institutions: Can Policy Changes Fix It?" *Online Journal of Distance Learning Administration*, 1998, 1(2). Retrieved Jan. 5, 2005, from http://www.westga.edu/~distance/ojdla/winter64/meyen64.htm.

Dutton, W. H., and Loader, B. D. "Competition and Collaboration in Online Distance Learning." In W. Dutton (ed.), *Digital Academe: The New Media and Institutions of Higher Education and Learning*. New York: Routledge, 2002.

Epper, R. M., and Garn, M. C. *Virtual College and University Consortia: A National Study*. Boulder, Colo.: State Higher Education Executive Officers, 2003.

Farrell, G. M. *The Development of Virtual Education: A Global Perspective*. Vancouver, B.C., Canada: Commonwealth of Learning, 1999.

Gellman-Danley, B., and Fetzner, M. J. "Asking the Really Tough Questions: Policy Issues for Distance Learning." *Online Journal of Distance Learning Administration*, 1998, 1(1). Retrieved Jan. 5, 2005, from http://www.westga.edu/~distance/danley11.html.

Hanna, D. E., and Associates. *Higher Education in an Era of Digital Competition*. Madison, Wis.: Atwood, 2000.

Johnson, M. J., Hanna, D., and Olcott, D. *Bridging the Gap: Leadership, Technology, and Organizational Change for University Deans and Chairpersons*. Madison, Wis.: Atwood, 2003.

Kennedy, T. "Online Distance Learning: An Idea for the Times." *EDUCAUSE Quarterly*, 2006, 4, 67–69.

King, J. W., and others. "Policy Frameworks for Distance Education: Implications for Decision Makers." *Online Journal of Distance Learning Administration*, 2000, 3(2). Retrieved Jan. 5, 2005, from http://www.westga.edu/~distance/king32.html.

McCoy, D. R. *A Policy Analysis of Selected Public Virtual Universities in the United States*. Unpublished doctoral dissertation, Northern Illinois University, 2002.

Merriam, S. B. *Case Study Research in Education: A Qualitative Approach*. San Francisco: Jossey-Bass, 1988.

Moore, M. G. *From Chautauqua to the Virtual University: A Century of Distance Education in the United States*. ERIC Clearinghouse on Adult, Career, and Vocational Education, Columbus, Ohio, 2003.

National Center for Educational Statistics. *Distance Education at Postsecondary Education Institutions: 2000–2001* (NCES 2003-017). Washington, D.C.: U.S. Department of Education, 2003.

Rosevear, S. G. "Lessons for Developing a Partnership-Based Virtual University." *Technology Source*, 1999. Retrieved Jan. 5, 2005, from http://ts.mivu.org/default.asp?show=article&id=30.

Smith, B. "Creating Consortia: Exporting the Best, Import the Rest." *Converge Magazine*, Dec. 1, 1998.

Twigg, C. A. *Expanding Access to Learning: The Role of Virtual Universities*. Troy, N.Y.: Center for Academic Transformation, 2003.

Wolf, D. B., and Johnstone, S. M. "Cleaning up the Language: Establishing a Consistent Vocabulary for Electronically Delivered Academic Programs." *Change, 31*(4), July/August 1999, 34–39.

Yin, R. K. *Case Study Research: Design and Methods* (2nd ed.). Thousand Oaks, Calif.: Sage, 1994.

HAIXIA XU *is a doctoral candidate in the Institute of Higher Education at the University of Georgia.*

LIBBY V. MORRIS *is professor and director of the Institute of Higher Education at the University of Georgia.*

NEW DIRECTIONS FOR HIGHER EDUCATION • DOI: 10.1002/he

7

State-level virtual institutions have taken various and instructive paths as they developed.

On the Edge of Innovation: Transition and Transformation in Statewide Administrative Models for Online Learning

Myk Garn

In November 1996, forty-five higher education technology leaders convened in Washington, D.C., to discuss the virtual university (VU). The future of higher education appeared to hang in the balance. The Western Governors Association had announced establishment of the Western Governors University (WGU). As a result, VU initiatives were emerging from, or being contemplated by, almost every state-level higher education administrator. "It was a feeling of 'Virtual university? Gotta have one!'" (personal communication with Dick Hezel, Feb. 8, 2008). Carol Twigg set the tone for the meeting: "To those who believe the current system is ossified and unreformable, this trend [of creating virtual universities] is an important catalyst for change in higher education" (Twigg and Oblinger, 1996, p. 15). Unlike the WGU (whose progenitors intended to establish a new *separate*, accredited, instructional entity), the initiatives in this chapter were established to catalyze and transform the existing institutions *within* their state's system of higher education. The focus on driving change to the existing system, rather than creating a new system, became the dominant response in the states. Fueled by the dot-com phenomenon, political and higher education leaders felt pressure to react to WGU. By 2003, at least sixty-one state-level virtual higher education entities had been established across

NEW DIRECTIONS FOR HIGHER EDUCATION, no. 146, Summer 2009 © Wiley Periodicals, Inc.
Published online in Wiley InterScience (www.interscience.wiley.com) • DOI: 10.1002/he.346

55

forty-five states (Epper and Garn, 2003, p. 5). Many models were under consideration, but few were as divergent as the WGU model. The ferment was moving rapidly.

Purposefully Different

California Virtual University, Florida Virtual Campus, Michigan Virtual University, and Kentucky Virtual University were not like WGU. They were not intended to be. The reform-minded WGU was clear in its intent to create a new institution not built from, or affiliated with, any traditional existing institution; these four entities (like almost all the other virtual colleges or universities initiated during this period) were intended to be embedded, and catalyze innovation, *within* the existing structures, powers, and politics of states' public higher education ecosystem. These statewide virtual learning entities reveal the key needs and roles for which each was established, how they changed over time, and the changes they made to survive.

California Virtual University (CVU). One of the most explicit expressions of this intent to change the existing system—and the challenges of doing so—came from the California Virtual University (CVU). CVU developed in direct response to creation of the WGU, which California Governor Pete Wilson declined to join. Reasoning California was large enough to support its own initiative, and that California did not want an external agency dictating the policies of its institutions, he created a committee that established CVU as an independent foundation in September 1997.

CVU embodied the essential differences between the WGU and the other initiatives: "The WGU effort has higher education reform at its philosophical roots" (Berg, 1998, p. 11). WGU was a multistate collaborative focused on establishing a directly competing, separately accredited, alternative academic marketplace and intended to embrace business as both a partner and a primary consumer. By contrast, CVU was intended to work within the existing system and would not be a direct provider of instruction or seek separate accreditation. Instead it would catalyze and support the efforts of existing institutions by establishing new relationships and services and recruiting traditional faculty into online teaching. In essence, the WGU intended to build a model that would establish and empower a new market of empowered learners while the CVU proposed to change the current system's ability to leverage technology to transform itself.

CVU was to provide a catalog of courses and programs from California's institutions, enabling a new generation of distance learning students. In addition, online services were planned so students could identify distance learning courses at other institutions and transfer credit to their home institution. The partners included the University of California system, California State University system, the community college system, and some private institutions, notably Stanford University and the University of Southern

NEW DIRECTIONS FOR HIGHER EDUCATION • DOI: 10.1002/he

California. During this phase, funding of $250,000 was contributed by the Alfred P. Sloan Foundation.

CVU staff worked with campus faculty senates to develop relationships, provide grants to develop courses and programs, and establish the CVU catalog, which eventually included more than a hundred institutions (or about 70 percent of all California public higher education institutions). The preliminary version of the online distance learning catalog went live in 1997.

CVU was challenged to find financial sustainability. Governor Wilson saw CVU as the digital melding of business and education. Seeking potential partners from the state's many high-tech firms, Wilson promoted the opportunity to establish new profit-making beachheads in the education sector. Ultimately, only five of ten targeted corporate sponsors (Oracle, Sun Microsystems, Cisco Systems, Pacific Bell, and International Thomson Publishing) signed on. Wilson also championed $16 million in state funding for online learning, including $6 million for CVU. However, when Republican Wilson lost to Democrat Gray Davis in the 1998 election, funding stalled.

CVU proposed several funding options, among them requesting $1 million a year from its institutional partners, seeking marketing opportunities (such as pop-up and banner ads on the CVU site), and selling textbooks. But the CVU's university partners rejected these options. Subsequently CVU, in formal operation for only eight months, ceased operation in March 1999. Later, California's community college system took over the CVU catalog, creating the California Virtual Campus with an annual budget of $2.9 million. By 2006, 136 accredited institutions in California were participating in CVU (Eduventures, 2006, p. 4).

Florida Virtual Campus. Announcements about WGU and CVU caught the attention of other state leaders and educators. In 1996, the Florida state legislature established the Florida Postsecondary Learning Institute, as a distance learning collaboration of the state's community college and university systems. The Institute was housed at the eLearning-oriented Florida Gulf Coast University in Ft. Myers. Intended to coordinate the two systems, the institute board consisted of four community college presidents, four university presidents, the chancellors of the two systems, a board member from each system, and the state Secretary of Administration. The proposed annual budget was $15 million.

Through 1997 and 1998, institute initiatives included developing an online catalog, implementing Teaching and Learning Technology Roundtables on campuses, and establishing an online reference librarian service. However, this momentum was dealt a blow in 1997 when only $500,000 was allocated instead of $15 million. A Virtual Institution Design Team was created in 1998 to design the core structure for a virtual campus framework, and in early 1999 it recommended creation of a Florida Virtual Campus (FVC). The recommendation was unanimously approved by the State Board of Community Colleges and Board of Regents, and the FVC was established on July 1, 1999. FVC funding included contributions by the state universities, the community colleges, and legislative appropriations. Shortly thereafter, the FVC was transferred to the newly created Florida Board of Education and relocated to the University of South Florida.

The Florida Distance Learning Consortium, established in 1996 by the State Board of Community Colleges, had been coordinating distance learning initiatives within the community college system, including developing and maintaining a separate online catalog. On July 1, 2003, the two initiatives merged to become the Florida Distance Learning Consortium (FDLC). This merger expanded the mission of the FDLC to provide "coordination in the development, delivery, marketing, and acquisition of distance learning instruction and its infrastructure across the K–20 system" (Petersons, n.d., para. 1).

Michigan Virtual University. The Michigan Virtual University (MVU) was established in 1998 by Governor John Engler and the Michigan Economic Development Corporation as a private, 501(c)(3) corporation. With direction to play an "aggressive" (Fitzpatrick, 1999, p. 1) role in developing and brokering online learning for education and training needs of industry, it was governed by a board of directors representing Michigan employers, education leaders, and state government. Start-up funding of $30 million over four years came from state workforce development funds.

Spencer and Fitzpatrick (2001, p. 3) described MVU as a public policy agency "accelerating the capacity of Michigan higher education institutions" by providing a "supportive 'incubator' environment," and serving as "key external catalysts to initiate campus-wide dialogs . . . surrounding virtual teaching and learning." The MVU would not seek academic accreditation, but it would "facilitate innovative and meaningful strategic partnerships with Michigan's 28 community colleges, 15 public four-year universities, and 43 independent colleges and universities" (Fitzpatrick, 1999, p. 1). MVU developed agreements through the Presidents Council (Michigan's equivalent of a statewide higher education coordinating body) with the state universities and partnered with the Virtual Learning Collaborative of the Michigan Community College Association.

MVU also established partnerships with several corporations, notably Ameritech, Consumers Energy, Steelcase, General Motors, Ford, and DaimlerChrysler. These relationships paid off with the Michigan Virtual Automotive College, launched in 1997, and creation of the Michigan Virtual Technology College in 1999. MVU used these entities and initiatives (such as establishing Oracle Internet Academies, furnishing online information technology courses from providers such as NETg, and an online career guidance system) to establish its business and training role.

In 2000, the Michigan legislature and governor appropriated an additional $18 million to MVU over three years to create and operate the Michigan Virtual High School (MVHS). MVHS was led by a coalition of K–12 education groups, including the Michigan Association of Secondary School

Administrators and the Michigan Education Association, the state's largest teachers union. The governor and legislature also approved $110 million in funding for a Teacher Technology Initiative to provide a personal computer, software, Internet access, and training for K–12 teachers across the state. The rollout and management of this initiative was given to the MVU/MVHS.

Over the next years, Michigan's economy slowed and MVU start-up investments were spent and not replaced with sufficient revenues. Also, with the passage of No Child Left Behind, the focus of MVU moved to meeting the online needs of Michigan's K–12 sector.

In October 2004, a significant change occurred. The majority of MVU's higher education programs were cancelled, the staff was reduced from sixty to thirty, and the MVU CEO changed. In 2005, the MVU was reorganized to focus on workforce training and K–12 activities: "With so much national attention on improving elementary and secondary schools, the shift in focus will be beneficial to students in Michigan" (Carnevale, 2004, p. A30). Although the title "Michigan Virtual University" remained, its mission statement now read: "Provide leadership in Michigan to increase student and educator access to diverse technology-based educational tools and resources that promote 21st Century learning skill for the general benefit of the K–12 community" (MVHS, 2005, p. i). In 2007, renamed the Michigan Virtual School, more than 27,000 course enrollments and some 150,000 students were served with online courses and services.

Kentucky Virtual University. In his December 1995 inaugural address, newly elected governor Paul E. Patton announced his intention to be known as Kentucky's higher education governor. Over the next eighteen months, he led a comprehensive reform of the state's postsecondary education system, including establishing the Kentucky Commonwealth Virtual University (KYVU) (Garn, 2005, p. 58).

Management of the initiative was placed under the state's higher education coordinating board, the Council on Postsecondary Education (CPE). A statewide Distance Learning Advisory Committee (DLAC) was established to guide the new entity. The DLAC was composed of public university presidents, the president of the Kentucky Community and Technical College System (KCTCS), the president of the Association of Independent Kentucky Colleges and Universities (AIKCU), three council members, and heads of several state agencies including the Department of Education.

CPE staff and statewide workgroups appointed by DLAC members developed the operational plan. The initial roles for KCVU were to (1) be a clearinghouse of institutional distance learning offerings, (2) use competency-based credentialing in support of workforce and professional development programs, and (3) serve as a single point of access to the Kentucky Virtual Library and academic support services for online learners.

The KCVU went live in fall 1999, supported by an annual allocation from the Kentucky General Assembly of approximately $1.6 million and with an additional $4.5 million for purchase of databases for the Kentucky Virtual

Library (Lozier, Oblinger, and Choa, 2002). The KYVU and KCTCS developed twenty-one online courses and established an online associate degree in business. This resulted in a core set of online general education courses that enabled KCTCS to add more than thirty programmatic options over the next few years. These programs, combined with KCTCS enrollment growth that went from about sixty thousand students in 1997 to more than ninety thousand in 2005, and the increasing offerings of Kentucky's other public postsecondary education institutions, became an engine of growth for KYVU.

This growth occurred even while KYVU was changing. After an initial multi-institutional collaboration on a course management system (CMS) in 1999, all of the public postsecondary institutions except KCTCS adopted their own campus-based licenses for alternative products by 2004. With excess infrastructure capacity, the KYVU formed support relationships with state agencies interested in online delivery of professional development programs. These included the Kentucky Department of Adult Education (which became part of the CPE in 2001) and the Education Professional Standards Board, the certifying agency for Kentucky's teachers.

Between 2002 and 2005, the initial KYVU staff of twenty and part of its budget were absorbed into CPE, thereby reducing resources and staff for daily operations. In May 2005, following a visit by the Southern Association of Colleges and Schools (SACS), a new strategic planning phase began. The results were both explicit (the KYVU changed its name to the Kentucky Virtual Campus) and implicit (the new organization committed itself to reengaging with the public postsecondary education institutions in addition to continuing to support online learning at state agencies). At this same time, KCTCS decided to purchase and manage its own CMS. As a result, even though use of the Virtual Campus catalog and the Kentucky Virtual Library remained strong, by mid-2008 KYVU CMS usage went from a high of sixty-five thousand users per term to fewer than ten thousand in primarily professional development courses. In addition, with state resources again reduced, the KYVU staff shrank to two individuals.

Terminal or Transitional?

These cases reveal how states envision, establish, and empower change-driving, transformative entities in higher education. Unlike WGU, each of these initiatives was embedded within—and intended to change—a state's existing postsecondary education system. Each underwent successive transitions attempting to find a symbiotic and sustainable role within its academic and political ecosystems. Since their creation, these change initiatives have themselves been transformed. The challenges, successes, and failures of each were unique, but they are also instructive to those who would seek to transform higher education. Some of the criteria Berg (1998) identified, like the brokering function, were common across the initiatives, while others (emphasis on training and sustainable funding) differentiate each entity.

The *brokering function* is the most obvious manifestation of the virtual ecosystem these entities were intended to create. Implemented as an online catalog with "one-stop shopping," this service afforded improved student access by aggregating listings from multiple institutions at a common Website. These catalogs manifested "collaboration" and addressed concerns of "unnecessary duplication," which support the argument that online technologies could increase the efficiency of higher education.

The degree to which a VCU worked with institutions developing academic programs online or with industry on workforce issues differentiates these entities. Two initiatives (CVU and MVU) saw relationships with, and reliance on, business as being the key. CVU had private industry as investors but took a traditional path focusing on institutions and faculty while the MVU sought industry partnerships for both funding and training. KYVU, in 1999–2001, acquired some credential programs and later supported GED, teacher training, and principal certification programs for other state agencies. But its primary focus remained fixed on higher education. FVU exhibited the most focus on higher education. It invested a majority of its effort with faculty and faculty senates to encourage adoption of new instructional models.

Establishing a viable financial structure independent of state funding has proven challenging. Most VUs needed ongoing external investments; only a few received them, and none could sustain them. Both CVU and MVU were explicitly intended to become self-supporting. CVU kicked off with up-front investment from industry and worked through a number of sustainability options. Governor Wilson proposed to leverage California's high-tech firms, that would join for $75,000 each, and championed $6 million in state funding. Later CVU proposed institutions contribute $1 million annually, but every proposal failed to garner support. With no viable funding model, CVU became an online catalog run by the community college system.

MVU received a three-year start-up allocation of workforce development funds after which it must be self-supporting. As a result, MVU pursued a greater range of potentially lucrative opportunities than the other VCUs. Several, including managing a statewide rollout of laptops to K–12 teachers and offering advanced placement courses, were substantially different from its initial focus. Eventually this resulted in a greater alignment with Michigan's K–12 community and their needs than those of higher education.

Conversely, the KYVU and FVU were dependent on allocations from state (KYVU) or system partners (FVU). KYVU was established in statute with a recurring allocation from Kentucky's General Assembly. These resources enabled it to engage in long-term planning and transition services as needs shifted. KYVU also established several potential revenue-producing projects, but these were never more than 5 percent of revenues in any year. Finally, although it did not feel pressure to be "profitable" (as did MVU and CVU), FVU did not get in the state budget, as did KYVU. As a result,

NEW DIRECTIONS FOR HIGHER EDUCATION • DOI: 10.1002/he

instead of adopting a change-driving role, the FVU assumed a supportive relationship with its consortia partners, resulting in an enduring presence in Florida's higher education institutions.

It seems clear that the greater the focus on external funding, the more tenuous sustainability is. Of the two entities that looked to private industry for investment and clients, CVU lost its independent momentum and MVU was subsumed by the Michigan Virtual High School. KYVU (now the Kentucky Virtual Campus) and the FVU (now the Florida Distance Learning Consortium) continue to evolve and impact their higher education ecosystems.

Other forces also drove change. A virtual institution's affinity with the state's community colleges and the rise of virtual K–12 schools were influencers, as was the impact of the champion (or the champion's departure). Community colleges were the most receptive higher education partner for a virtual institution. In California, the community college system took over CVU and carried the online catalog once the management structure collapsed. In Florida, the community college system incorporated FVU during a reorganization in 2003. In Kentucky, when the universities stopped using the KYVU course management system, the community college system used KYVU services and program development loan funds to become the state's leading provider of distance learning courses and programs.

Over time, the emergence of momentum for K–12 virtual initiatives competed with some VCUs and dramatically changed the Michigan Virtual University. States paid increased attention to K–12 issues with the passage of No Child Left Behind in 2001. NCHEMS (2006) identified growth in K–12 virtual schools as competing for time and funding from political leaders. This impact was greatest for the MVU. Describing its reorganization in 2004–05, the new CEO stated, "One could argue a good portion of our work is done in [the higher education] area. . . . Higher education around the country has evolved in [such] a way that it has become more campus-based. Most online education is now developed on individual campuses instead of through a group of institutions working together" (Carnevale, 2004, p. A30).

The impact of a champion was most universal and significant. Champions introduced these potentially transformative entities into traditional academia. All four of these VUs resulted from explicit intentions and actions on the part of a champion. In three cases, the champion was a governor, in the fourth a college president. Each was motivated to provide state-level alternatives to WGU, to meet the policy needs of the time, and establish leadership that was recognized nationally. The champions charged these entities to be self-sustaining change mechanisms *within* their respective systems.

This very visible political support had a powerful effect on the initial phase of these VUs. Some were good. Governor Patton endowed the KYVU with significant political capital and funding, as did Governor Engler for MVU and (to a lesser extent) Governor Wilson for CVU. Some were not.

NEW DIRECTIONS FOR HIGHER EDUCATION • DOI: 10.1002/he

When Wilson left office, funding from industry (leveraged personally by Wilson) dried up, and requests to the institutions and the legislature went cold. In Michigan, when Engler left office, Michigan's K–12 administration asserted influence over MVU. FVU experienced change as a result of the turbulent restructuring of Florida's higher education system in the late 1990s and early 2000s. Ultimately, each VU had to find a way to survive after its champion moved on.

These state-level public VUs were both an alternative to the external WGU and a catalyst to initiate and drive the use of online instruction within the state's academic ecosystem. They showcased the leadership of its champion and empowered the innovators within higher education so they could address issues of access, affordability, and efficiency through new uses of the Internet.

Evolution within a system is perilous. When the champion left or funding streams waned, the VUs changed their focus and goals. Clearly, each must establish its own role and ongoing funding, or it would perish. Embedded, traditionally funded initiatives (such as KYVU and FVU) transitioned more successfully than the more independently envisioned and funded entities (CVU and MVU).

Now, more than ever, higher education needs catalytic and disruptive entities. VUs played a significant role in engaging, preparing, and providing options for, and response to, the entry of virtual learning into the academic ecosystem of their respective states. Although initially a manifestation of political will, these VUs fostered valuable attention and energy during a time of change. They engaged with student, faculty and institutional constituencies, increasing the awareness, amount of, and access to online courses and programs. They were a common ground across institutional boundaries to convene, discuss, and coordinate during a time of significant change.

References

Berg, G. A. "Public Policy on Distance Learning in Higher Education: California State and Western Governors Association Initiatives." *Education Policy Analysis Archives*, 1998, 6(11). Retrieved Dec. 23, 2008, from http://epaa.asu.edu/epaa/v6n11.html.

Carnevale, D. "Michigan Virtual U. Shifts Its Focus to Elementary and Secondary Schools." *Chronicle of Higher Education*, Nov. 5, 2004, A30.

Eduventures. *Performance Indicators for State/System Online Higher Education Consortia.* May 2006, Catalog no. 5OHECRR0506.

Epper, R. M., and Garn, M. *Virtual College and University Consortia: A National Study.* Boulder, Colo.: State Higher Education Executive Officers, 2003.

Fitzpatrick, J. T. "Michigan Virtual University Update." Michigan Association for Computer Users in Learning (MACUL) newsletter, Mar., 1999.

Garn, M. A. *Power, Politics, and the 1997 Restructuring of Higher Education Governance in Kentucky.* Dissertation, University of Kentucky, 2005.

Lozier, G., Oblinger, D., and Choa, M. "Organizational Models for Delivering Distance Learning." EDUCAUSE Center for Applied Research, Research Bulletin, 2002(2).

Michigan Virtual High School (MVHS). *Report to the Michigan Department of Education on the Development and Growth of the Michigan Virtual High School.* Apr. 13, 2005.

Retrieved Dec. 16, 2008, from http://www.mivhs.org/upload_2/MDE_Development andGrowth_MVHS1999-2005.pdf.

National Center for Higher Education Management Systems (NCHEMS). *Kentucky Virtual University Environmental Scan*. Boulder, Colo.: Author, 2006.

Petersons. Florida Distance Learning Consortium, n.d. Retrieved Dec. 16, 2008, from http://www.petersons.com/distancelearning/code/consortiaidd.asp?inunId=138660& sponsor=13.

Spencer, D. A., and Fitzpatrick, J. T. "Hearing on Technology and Education," Mar. 8, 2001. Prepared witness testimony, U.S. House of Representatives Committee on Energy and Commerce.

Twigg, C., and Oblinger, D. *The Virtual University*. Report from Joint Educom/IBM Roundtable. Washington, D.C.: Educom, 1996.

MYK GARN *is director of the Educational Technology Cooperative at the Southern Regional Education Board. From 1999 through 2008, he worked as chief academic officer for the Kentucky Virtual University and then as executive director of the Kentucky Virtual Campus.*

NEW DIRECTIONS FOR HIGHER EDUCATION • DOI: 10.1002/he

8

The closing of the U.S. Open University provides lessons that may be relevant to other institutions of higher education creating new online initiatives.

A Review of the Short Life of the U.S. Open University

Lynette M. Krenelka

How can a virtual university go from founding to closing in three years? This chapter presents the findings of a single case study of the United States Open University (USOU), including factors affecting its demise and success. Interviews were conducted with administrators, board members, associate faculty, and staff who played a major role in the planning and operation of the USOU and pertinent documents reviewed. By studying USOU's short life from 1998 to 2002, many lessons can be learned that may be relevant to other institutions of higher education entering new online endeavors.

Background and Historical Perspective

The U.S. Open University (USOU) was developed during a time of explosive growth in online education in the United States and also during a weakened economy leading to the dot-com bust. Reasons for the bust were overestimates of the market's size, the entry of new education suppliers, and subsequent fierce competition (Meyer, 2003).

The USOU was incorporated in 1998 as an independent, private higher education institution with not-for-profit status. Developed as a sister institution to the UK Open University of Milton Keynes in the United Kingdom, USOU adopted (and extended) the mission of the UK Open University (OU), as well as the teaching system pioneered by the OU, called "supported open learning." This model focused on learning outcomes, personal support to students from associate faculty, high-quality course materials based on research-based pedagogy, and well-organized logistics. Students

NEW DIRECTIONS FOR HIGHER EDUCATION, no. 146, Summer 2009 © Wiley Periodicals, Inc.
Published online in Wiley InterScience (www.interscience.wiley.com) • DOI: 10.1002/he.347

were encouraged to become independent learners (Distance Education and Training Council Accreditation Commission, 2001). USOU's concept statement states:

> United States Open University provides a world-class educational choice to self-motivated students who want a personal, accessible and flexible learning experience. USOU's proven Supported Open Learning method combines high-quality multi-media learning materials, personalized faculty support and peer interaction, with online technologies that enable students to study when and where their schedules permit.

The goal of USOU was to furnish the last two years of an undergraduate degree as well as a master's degree. All funding was provided and approved through the OU board.

Administratively, USOU was tied to the OU through Sir John Daniel, vice chancellor of the OU, who also served as president of USOU's Board of Governance. Sir John lent the vision for USOU and was the sole liaison to the OU board. USOU had two physical offices, one in Denver, Colorado, and another in Wilmington, Delaware. The Denver office housed the higher-level administrators (the chancellor, vice chancellor/controller, vice chancellor of academic affairs, director of learning, director of recruitment/marketing, Web support staff). The Wilmington office held the vice chancellor of educational services and all of the student support services staff. The two offices worked well together as an organization.

Events happened quickly. In June 1998, USOU was incorporated. By September 1999, a chancellor was hired. In February 2000, USOU's first U.S.-based pilot semester was started, with seven courses, eighty-nine students, and nine associate faculty. By summer and fall 2000, student services staff were hired and a student help desk was implemented. In June 2001, Sir John Daniel resigned from his position at OU. By January 2002, USOU was closed.

Factors Affecting Closure

Many factors led to the closing of the USOU. Some of them are a business plan with unrealistic enrollment projections; lack of regional accreditation and federal financial aid; a poor fit between USOU and OU structures; difficulty with marketing online offerings in a national market with limited funds; funding that was short-term, undercapitalized, and restricted to one source; and loss of a visionary leader (Krenelka, 2005).

Business Plan with Unrealistic Projections. The USOU business plan developed by OU presented several challenges. The enrollment projections in the USOU business plan were based on OU courses, which had very high enrollments. Enrollment was set at two thousand for the first year and six thousand the second year. One board member said, "The business plan was

New Directions for Higher Education • DOI: 10.1002/he

based on enrollment numbers and was prepared by the British who had never been involved in launching a new effort in the United States" (Krenelka, 2005, p. 81). Another administrator added, "There was no basis for the estimates, the estimates were always too high, we were always failing" (p. 81). Although the administration and staff of the USOU worked very hard to meet enrollment projections, the goals were never realized. In fact, the administrators spent a great deal of time constantly modifying the business plan. The initial business plan was also one of the five problems faced by the USOU's chancellor, Richard Jarvis: "The initial business plans for the USOU perhaps had too much emphasis on academic goals rather than business ones, and a precarious funding base that relied on student tuition for so much of its working capital" (Meyer, 2006, p. 6).

Lack of Regional Accreditation and Limited Federal Financial Aid. USOU lacked regional accreditation; therefore U.S. companies would not reimburse the tuition costs of employees taking USOU courses (Krenelka, 2005; Meyer, 2006). Although work was begun immediately to obtain regional accreditation through the Middle States Association of Colleges and Schools, the only accreditation USOU received before its closing was through the Distance Education and Training Council (DETC) in mid-2001. DETC's accreditation did open some doors because some companies allowed their employees to use tuition reimbursement for USOU courses, but it did not carry the same prestige of regional accreditation. Students wanted to enroll in an institution that was regionally accredited so they could easily transfer USOU credits to other institutions.

Another factor that affected enrollment was limited financial aid available for part-time students; aid was available to full-time students or those enrolled in at least twelve semester credit hours. The 50 Percent Rule, implemented in 1992, prevented an institution from participating in Title IV federal financial aid programs if its distance learning courses (be they telecommunications or correspondence courses) exceeded 50 percent of the total classes offered.

Fitting the USOU Structure into the OU Structure. To save money and time, OU structures were used as a foundation for the USOU. For example, the OU's antiquated learning management system was thought to be adequate for USOU. After some consideration, the USOU board and administration decided to find a new learning management system, which took time to research and implement. Another difference was OU course materials, which were traditional correspondence or paper-based, when USOU was moving into online education. The length and depth of courses also differed. The UK courses were sixteen-credit courses offered over an entire year; the USOU courses were usually three- to-four-credit courses offered over a sixteen-week semester. In addition, linguistic differences delayed USOU's course offerings, as terms incorporated into OU courses were British-based and needed to be removed from USOU courses; again, this took time. Also,

USOU began development of online student support services different from the paper-based OU model for admission, registration, and payment. In the end, the many changes (new learning management system, modifications to OU original course materials and length of course offerings, and development of online student support services) took a great deal of time but were necessary to better fit the U.S. educational model and the online environment (Krenelka, 2005).

Marketing Online Offerings in a National Market with Limited Funds. How do you effectively market online courses in a national market with limited funding? Clearly, this is difficult. There are no national media vehicles for marketing national programs. To add to an already difficult job, USOU was a new entity without brand recognition. So marketing USOU required both developing brand recognition and recruiting students. One administrator summed up the marketing challenges with these words: "We were trying to achieve so much with so little in a country that is very diverse, its media is extraordinarily fragmented and it is a very competitive environment." For student recruitment, the USOU focused on regional and targeted local marketing efforts, owing to limited funds. Course pricing was not an issue for USOU because it was competitive with undergraduate tuition and charged $210 per undergraduate credit and $315 per credit for graduate tuition. However, USOU did not have brand recognition, and there was strong competition from many other providers for online learning in the United States.

Funding That Was Short-Term, Undercapitalized, and Restricted to One Source. Funding for the USOU was controlled by the OU board. Each year, USOU administrators would put together a breakeven budget based on enrollment. Thanks to low enrollment, revenue from tuition was $32,000 in 1999 and $75,303 in 2000. Expenses were $1.7 million in 1999 and $4.6 million in 2000. During this time period, the OU was facing changes in the UK education system and a more competitive environment; therefore, OU was increasingly reluctant to continue increasing its funding contribution. USOU administrators then began conversation with additional funding sources (such as foundations, international organizations, publishing companies, educational institutions). But the OU was reluctant to accept financial partners because this meant loss of overall control of the USOU.

Loss of a Visionary Leader. Sir John Daniel was a visionary leader for USOU, and he also served as direct liaison to the OU board. In spring 2001, he resigned his position. It is difficult to know whether USOU might have survived if Sir John had stayed as its top administrator and liaison to the OU. However, it might have been different if there had been more than one champion with connections to the OU board.

Elements of Success

Even though it closed in a short period of time, the USOU had several positive aspects that are worth mentioning. The administrators and staff of

USOU were extremely proud of what USOU had accomplished in just a few years. They felt, given more time, they would have met enrollment projections and would have secured additional funding. USOU associate faculty and staff reported that students were satisfied with all aspects of USOU, including course materials and student services. In fact, students returned and enrolled in multiple courses. Students felt that USOU staff had a strong, positive relationship with them. The administration of USOU was very involved and committed to the organization and modeled participatory leadership throughout the organization. Weekly conference calls were held to gather input from staff. Another positive factor of USOU was that associate faculty members were very student-focused and forward-thinking and were always incorporating new ideas into online learning. In addition, enrollment of the USOU was increasing, but not at the rapid pace initially set in the business plan by OU representatives.

Lessons Learned

Lessons learned from establishing (and closing) USOU are important for others contemplating virtual institutions. Lessons learned throughout the short life of the USOU include extending the advocacy role to more than one person, incorporating multiple sources of funding, developing the business plan with experts, partnering with strong academic institutions, starting with a large marketing budget for national online programs, allowing enough time for start-up initiatives, gaining regional accreditation early, and starting small with a few degrees and then expanding.

Extend Advocacy Role to Others. Do not rely on one person to serve as advocate or champion for the organization. Even though the visionary leader or champion may not have any plans to leave the organization, it could happen. Involve others in the advocacy role to the organization(s) that provide funding or governance. If a group of individuals serve as advocates for the virtual university and if one advocate leaves, the institution maintains advocates who can continue to develop strong relationships with partners, funders, and boards.

Incorporate Multiple Sources of Funding. Depending on only one source of funding may have contributed to the quick closing of USOU. Therefore, a single funding source may be too risky. If that source is diminished, problems arise. If multiple funding sources are in place, the financial burden is spread out and the loss of one funding source may not be devastating to the organization. It is unknown whether USOU would have been successful in securing additional funding sources; it was closed before this could happen.

Develop the Business Plan with Experts. The initial business plan for USOU was developed primarily by OU representatives and based on the OU experience. The enrollment projections in the business plan were extremely high, because the OU was very successful and achieved high enrollment in its courses. The U.S. market was quite different. The United States has several thousand competitors in the online education market, which target nearly the same student population.

Partner with Strong Academic Institutions. USOU found the highest rate of success (and the largest enrollments) from students enrolling from the partner higher education institutions. One example was with the University of Maryland Baltimore County, which partnered with USOU in offering a master's of information systems online. Partnering with strong academic institutions also eased the marketing challenge because students were familiar with and loyal to the partner institution. One issue to consider in establishing partnerships is admission standards. The USOU required a minimum GPA of 2.5, and one of its partners had a GPA requirement of 3.0. USOU staff worked with the partner institution to gain provisional status for its students so they could enroll.

Start with a Large Marketing Budget for National Online Programs. Marketing an online, national program is very expensive. USOU tried a variety of media, including television, radio, Web-based advertising, and print such as newspaper, journals, and newsletters, but it did not have sufficient resources for a national campaign.

Start-up Initiatives Take Time. It takes a minimum of five years for a new, start-up organization to break even or be considered successful. USOU was operational for only three years. Three years is not enough time to determine a start-up company's success.

Regional Accreditation Plays a Major Role in Higher Education. Students are looking for regionally accredited schools and curricula. Without regional accreditation, they are reluctant to enroll in the institution (Arnone, 2002; Krenelka, 2005). This is also important because companies reimburse tuition for employees only if the institution is regionally accredited.

Start Small by Offering a Few Degrees; Once Successful, Then Expand. If a virtual university tries to be all things to all people, it may not be successful because it has too many offerings to market and too many degree programs to administer, and it may not have enough resources to cover all activities. As administrators reflected on the offerings of USOU, many felt that USOU should have offered a few strong master's-level degree programs and then expanded into other academic areas.

It is helpful to evaluate USOU using Carchidi's adaptation cycle of virtual postsecondary education organizations (2002). The cycle is (1) matching markets to organizational capacity, (2) designing systems that connect markets to capacity, (3) managing the system, and (4) legitimizing the system and its products. Carchidi suggests that

> successful organizations are those that possess a more textured understanding of their place within the market, their learners and their internal capacity. It seems that organizations that have more highly developed marketing research functions are better able to understand the market and the place of the organization's products within it [2002, p. 198].

USOU suffered from several problems in each of the four cycles or phases, which happened quickly. In the first phase of matching, it lost its organizational champion (Sir John Daniel moved on), never forged successful revenue streams (revenue was cut off from the OU to the USOU), and had a competitive relationship with its founding organization (OU formed USOU as a sister institution, using it as a foundation and funding source). In the designing phase, the largest issue was lack of financial aid and accreditation for USOU. In the managing phase, the issues included historical policies of OU (which required that USOU take additional time to make changes, such as adding a new learning management system and online student services), control of course and program development process by the OU, and a change in organizational champion (the loss of Sir John). In the final phase of legitimizing its product and system, problems occurred with distinctiveness of product (the online market was growing and USOU did not have a unique product), marketing challenges (USOU was not known as a national online institution), ties to a higher-status organization (strict ties of USOU to OU made it difficult to incorporate additional funding sources), and external recognition (there was no brand recognition of the OU in the United States; therefore, marketing USOU was difficult). In other words, USOU had many problems to overcome at each stage of adaptation.

Closing

There is no way of knowing if USOU would have been successful in reaching its enrollment targets if it had not closed so quickly. Would additional funding sources have prevented the closing? It is difficult to predict. Also, could additional advocacy of USOU representatives rather than relying on one person have prolonged the life of USOU? It is likely that no one factor led to the closing of USOU, but it was the result of a combination of many factors. However, the lessons learned can be helpful to new higher education institutions wishing to begin a new venture, whether it is online or not.

References

Arnone, M. "United States Open U to Close After Spending $20 Million." *Chronicle of Higher Education,* 2002, *48*(23), A44.

Carchidi, D. (2002). *The Virtual Delivery and Virtual Organization of Postsecondary Education.* New York: Routledge Falmer, 2002.

Distance Education and Training Council Accreditation Commission. *US Open University Self-Study Report.* Feb. 2001.

Krenelka, L. *A Case Study of the Short Life of the US Open University: Perspectives of Administrators, Board Members, Associate Faculty and Staff.* Doctoral dissertation, University of North Dakota, Grand Forks, May 2005.

New Directions for Higher Education • DOI: 10.1002/he

Meyer, K. A. "The Rule of the Marketplace: Flawed Assumptions Contributed to the Failure of Dot-coms and VU's." *EDUCAUSE Quarterly*, 2003, 2, 4–7.
Meyer, K. A. "The Closing of the US Open University." *EDUCAUSE Quarterly*, 2006, 2, 5–7.

LYNETTE M. KRENELKA is director of academic planning of online and distance education at the University of North Dakota.

NEW DIRECTIONS FOR HIGHER EDUCATION • DOI: 10.1002/he

Different funding models have been used to fund virtual universities.

The Funding of Virtual Universities

Russell Poulin, Demarée K. Michelau

> Politics is the art of the possible.
>
> —Otto Von Bismarck

> Politics is not the art of the possible. It consists in choosing between the disastrous and the unpalatable.
>
> —John Kenneth Galbraith

Virtual universities are political creatures. Each virtual university (VU) has been created to address the unique set of needs and political forces that existed at its inception. Some VUs definitely reflect the "art of the possible," as a set of institutions band together to achieve goals they could not reach on their own. Other VUs were created by fiat by legislatures or governing/coordinating boards to avoid the "disastrous" (such as continuing to leave some populations unserved, developing incompatible networks or services, duplicating expensive services) in favor of the "unpalatable" (loss of institutional autonomy, or the difficulties of multi-institutional coordination). VUs reflect the diverse set of local political and financial atmospheres in which they were formed. Not surprisingly, their funding models are also diverse.

This chapter reviews categorization models and the outcomes of a VU funding survey (Michelau and Poulin, 2008). Although categorization of types of funding mechanisms is a necessary analytical tool, it often hides the many and varied political decisions that created them. In commenting on

the implications of the type of funding model, political forces behind the choice of a particular model are discussed in select cases. How a political organization (legislatures, state or provincial systems, and institutions) distributes its funding is often the most obvious evidence of its priorities.

Virtual University Organizational and Funding Taxonomies

In 1998, when electronic virtual universities were first flourishing, Wolf and Johnstone (1999) sought to develop a consistent taxonomy for categorizing these types of organization:

- Type 1 Degree-granting
- Type 2 Centralized student services and academic articulation
- Type 3 Limited services; little or no articulation
- Type 4 Electronic course catalog; few or no services; no articulation

The proposed categories were based on the combination of services offered and the complexity of interinstitutional agreements employed by the virtual university. The purpose of this taxonomy was to obtain a handle on the types of organizations being observed and created in a time of rapid development of VUs.

This taxonomy is less useful for analyzing financial models. Although a more complex organization might imply the need for more funding, this taxonomy masks the intricacies of the sources and levels of funding.

Epper and Garn (2003) conducted a survey that outlined many of the characteristics of VUs. From their findings, they expanded on the Wolf and Johnstone taxonomy to create the two-dimensional taxonomy in Table 1.

From a funding standpoint, Epper and Garn's revised taxonomy improves on earlier models by introducing the importance of the business model into understanding how a VU operates. This addition reflects the changes in the services offered and the funding sources of these organizations since the Wolf and Johnstone taxonomy was developed. In 1999, many of the multi-institutional consortia were still mostly funded by grants or legislative start-up funds. As time passed, they developed additional funding sources to support their activities.

Shortly after the release of the Epper and Garn work, James Mingle (former president of the State Higher Education Executive Officers) conducted a review of financing models for electronic consortia (Mingle, 2003). Mingle categorized consortia (see list above) by their primary sources of revenue. Although several of the organizations received funding from more than one source, categorizing by the primary source of funding helped clarify how each VU operated.

Table 1. Virtual University Organizational Taxonomy

	Low Business Practice	High Business Practice
High centralization	*Central agency model:* provides central student services and academic articulation. Organizationally and financially embedded in an academic agency, such as a system office or coordinating board.	*Central enterprise model:* provides central student services and academic articulation. May be organizationally embedded in an academic agency, but behaves as a business enterprise by building revenue streams for self-sustainability and engaging in quality control and performance measurement.
Low centralization	*Distributed agency model:* provides electronic course catalog; few or no services; no articulation. Organizationally and financially embedded in an academic agency, such as a system office or coordinating board.	*Distributed enterprise model:* provides electronic course catalog; few or no services; no articulation. May be organizationally embedded in an academic agency, but engages in limited business practices, such as quality control, performance measurement, standardization, and benchmarking.

Source: Epper and Garn (2003).

Virtual University Funding Taxonomy

Direct State Appropriations. The state appropriates funding directly to the consortium. A defined set of services are provided "free" to participating institutions.

Member Fee Organizations. Member institutions pay a fee or dues to support the operations of the consortium and its collaborative activities.

Tuition Revenue Sharing Plan. The tuition and fees charged to a student are divided according to preset formula among (1) the home institution where the student matriculates and receives credit; (2) the provider (or teaching) institution that offers the course to students throughout the consortium; and (3) a centralized unit that supports the operations of the consortium.

Informal Consortia. Usually started by a grant, the operations of the consortia are primarily donated. The "real collaboration" is at the faculty level, often without an exchange of dollars.

Private Sector Model. Funding would come from fees, services, and capital from the private sector. Some institutions and states created for-profit spin-offs.

How Are Virtual Universities Funded?

In 2008, the Western Cooperative for Educational Telecommunications (WCET) and the Western Interstate Commission for Higher Education (WICHE) conducted the first in-depth survey on funding of virtual universities. Initial drafts of the survey were pilot-tested by representatives of VUs, who provided valuable feedback in refining the questions. Here are highlights from the survey results. Note that all funding amounts are for academic year 2007. Of the thirty-nine respondents, seven are from organizations that operated "cross-border" (in multiple states or provinces), and three are Canadian organizations.

The annual operating budget (see Table 2) for the VUs varies greatly. Only one-third operate with a budget greater than $1 million and nearly half have an annual budget of less than $500,000. Considering the amount spent on higher education in these states or provinces, the budgets for these VUs are not very large and support only a handful of staff.

Respondents were asked to report their exact level of funding in each of several funding categories. The following paragraphs include highlights from the survey, comments on their responses, and observations on each funding category.

State/provincial appropriations (not grants). For the organizations that serve a single state or province, nearly 40 percent received no appropriation. This is surprising; these organizations tend to promote collaboration and efficiencies for government-supported institutions. Nine of the VUs received appropriations of more than $1 million. As will be further explored, the appropriations for VUs remained relatively flat over previous years, with a few notable exceptions.

Federal appropriations (not grants). No VU reported direct federal appropriations. This finding is expected because higher education governance and funding in both the United States and Canada have been the responsibility of the states and provinces.

Dues from member institutions, schools, organizations. Dues are a fixed yearly payment from institutions to support services they receive from the

Table 2. Annual Budget of Virtual University Central Administrative Units

	Single State/Province	Cross-Border
Less than $500,000	14 (43.8%)	5 (71.4%)
$500,000–$1 million	5 (15.6%)	1 (14.3%)
$1,000,001–$3 million	7 (21.9%)	1 (14.35)
$3,000,001–$5 million	1 (3.1%)	0 (0.0%)
$5,000,001–$8 million	3 (9.4%)	0 (0.0%)
More than $8 million	2 (6.3%)	0 (0.0%)

Source: Michelau and Poulin (2008).

NEW DIRECTIONS FOR HIGHER EDUCATION • DOI: 10.1002/he

VU. One-third of the single state/province VUs collect dues, while nearly all (six of seven) of the cross-border respondents rely on dues. The first two funding categories, appropriations and dues, constitute the bulk of the funding for many of the VUs surveyed. For the VUs that primarily relied on appropriations or dues, the other funding categories (see below) either were not used or provided supplementary funding.

Revenue sharing for students registering for courses that are part of the consortium. In revenue-sharing agreements, the VU typically collects a percentage of the income generated from each enrollment to support its services. Only five of the organizations used revenue sharing; two of them received substantial funding. Colorado Community Colleges Online (CCCOnline) collected more than $8 million. Unlike other VUs, CCCOnline pays faculty costs, and much of the revenue is passed through to the faculty. Great Plains IDEA collected more than $1 million in revenue sharing. For both CCCOnline and Great Plains IDEA, students pay a premium for their courses. The total of tuition and fees is higher than for a similar on-campus course. The Illinois Internet Course Exchange is an example of a VU in which revenue sharing is used while not charging a premium price to students.

Per-course or per-credit fees for students registering for courses that are part of the consortium. Ten of the organizations surveyed used per-course or per-credit fees. Two of these organizations used both revenue sharing and per-course or per-credit fees. For twenty-six of the thirty-nine organizations, students were not asked to directly participate in the funding of the VU. This may change in the future, as other VUs follow the lead of Kentucky Virtual Campus, which implemented a per-course fee in 2008. Revenue sharing and student enrollment fees are viewed as ways to keep pace with burgeoning online enrollments and to overcome the inherent time lag of appropriations and dues that fund the services necessary to meet the demand.

Fees for services or sales or licensing of products developed or marketed by the consortium. In this category, services included seminar registrations, contracted instructional design, contracted multimedia design and development, and charges for hosting courses on central servers. Examples of sales and licensing were Connecticut Distance Learning Consortium's eTutoring and Minnesota State Colleges and Universities' eFolio. Fifteen of the VUs reported income from these two revenue streams. Only four respondents developed this into a substantial source of income with reported earnings of more than $300,000. The Connecticut Distance Learning Consortium has been an entrepreneurial leader, generating $700,000 from fees for services and an additional $150,000 by selling or licensing products. Fees for services and products may be a more popular source of funding in the future. Constrained budgets may force cutbacks on appropriations or dues payments. Fees for service can help maintain valued services or develop new services on a proof-of-concept basis.

Grants. Only ten respondents reported any income from grants, and only two of those grants were for more than $500,000 in fiscal year 2007. It is notable that only three grants were from private foundations. With distance education no longer being considered cutting-edge and with several private foundations turning their attention from higher education to K–12 needs, there are fewer sources for grant funding. Five federal grants were reported from four sources. The increase in congressional set-asides in the United States during this decade has decimated the U.S Department of Education's Fund for the Improvement of Postsecondary Education (FIPSE), which was once a rich source for grants to implement innovative practices in higher education.

Donated or in-kind services. Examples of these kinds of services include staff not charged to the consortium, office space, and server space. Eight virtual universities reported in-kind services. Of those, six reported income of less than $100,000, one reported a figure slightly higher, and one responded that the value of the donated services was unknown.

Other funding. Only three responses were recorded in the "other funding" category, suggesting that the previous categories adequately covered the main sources of income.

Observations and Conclusions

In reviewing the VU taxonomies, the results of the 2008 survey of VUs, and from experience working with VUs, we recommend a number of observations to anyone considering alternative methods for funding VUs.

There Is No One Best Financial Model. Governance and funding of higher education in the United States and Canada have been relegated to the states and provinces. The resulting governance and funding structures have local idiosyncrasies resulting from a mixture of history, leadership, educational needs, geographies, politics, and economies. Here is a review of some very different, but all successful, organizational models:

- *A confederation of members.* The Florida Distance Learning Consortium is a membership organization that has opened its ranks from only community colleges to accepting all colleges and universities in the state. Membership is voluntary. Members direct the activities. Funding is from dues, sales of services, and grants.
- *A highly centralized organization.* The Utah Education Network provides public television, videoconferencing, and Internet connectivity to all colleges and K–12 schools throughout the state. The state's institutions offer courses and programs over the networks. Funding is primarily from state appropriations.
- *A hybrid approach.* The Connecticut Distance Learning Consortium is part of a state agency, but membership by the state's public and private institutions is voluntary. The emphasis has been less on centralization and

more on gaining multi-institution efficiencies or advancements. Funding has been diverse: appropriations, dues, fees for service, sales of products, and grants.

The VU funding model should reflect the local situation and emphasize funding for services that will add value to the offerings of its member institutions. Successful VU leadership also understands that the list of services considered to be valuable changes over time.

The leaders of a VU must understand the political underpinnings that have an impact on fiscal decisions. Working as a consultant in the start-up of a systemwide VU in one state, one of the authors realized there was a historical barrier to institutions working in concert. Several years earlier, one institution conducted a political end run to gain additional funding. The administrators who remained from when that incident happened were wary about trusting colleagues at the institution that performed the end run. Additional safeguards were required to assure that the interinstitutional funding agreements would not be broken.

Diversify Your Funding Sources. In reflecting on the examples of VU funding models, James Mingle said, "None of the cases discussed are purely one 'type' or another. In fact, the most successful consortia appear to be those that depend on multiple sources of revenue rather than a single source" (Mingle, 2003, p. 3). This statement echoes the advice often given by financial advisors to diversify investment portfolios. If one source of income is lagging, other sources may be reaping economic benefits.

In reviewing the results of the 2008 survey of VUs (see Table 3), one sees that less than one-third of single state/province respondents had three or more sources of funding. There is a dichotomy among the cross-border collaborations. Considering that the VU with two funding sources received less than 1 percent of its funding from the second source, this implies that three cross-border collaborations receive all (or almost all) of their funding from one source. Four of them have three sources of funding.

It is also interesting to note that just over one-quarter (eleven of the thirty-nine) of those surveyed have only one funding source. Relying on

Table 3. Number of Funding Sources

Number of Sources	Single State/Province	Cross-Border
1	9 (28.1%)	2 (28.6%)
2	13 (40.6%)	1 (14.3%)
3	7 (21.9%)	4 (57.1%)
4	2 (6.3%)	0 (0.0%)
5	1 (3.1%)	0 (0.0%)

Source: Michelau and Poulin (2008).

NEW DIRECTIONS FOR HIGHER EDUCATION • DOI: 10.1002/he

only one funding source puts the organization at risk. When GeorgiaGlobe lost its legislative appropriation, it had no other source of funding and ceased to exist. The California Virtual University was a collaboration of the state's three higher education sectors; once the leader who crafted the vision for that VU departed, the California community colleges were left as the only sector willing to continue funding. Today, it is reborn as the California Virtual Campus, with a successful but different mission. Without multiple sources of funding, it is difficult to weather the political storms.

The Connecticut Distance Learning Consortium (CTDLC), with its five revenue streams, is a model entrepreneurial organization. Building on legislative appropriations and member dues, the consortium has been active in obtaining grant funding. CTDLC has developed services that are sold only to members. It has also expanded successful e-portfolio and e-tutoring products to other states, thus accumulating revenue outside of Connecticut.

Standardization Leads to Volume Leads to Income. Epper and Garn (2003) concluded that although there were superior performers from all four virtual college or university (VCU) categories, the "central enterprise" VCUs reported the highest overall success at meeting their goals. The central enterprise VCUs were self-sustaining or planned to become self-sustaining. These VCUs placed a higher funding emphasis on service fees (from institutions) and revenue sharing (partial tuition), both of which supply revenue streams tied to volume. The central enterprise VCUs were the most likely to take an active role in promoting standardization and scalability of instruction, addressing the issues that might dramatically increase (or impede) growth of VCU enrollments, and thus revenues tied to that growth.

Rhonda Epper is now co-director of Colorado Community Colleges Online (CCCOnline), which has developed a funding model that relies solely on revenue sharing. By developing quality expectations of their faculty, standard technologies, and ubiquitous student services, they have lowered the barriers to institutional and student participation. With the additional enrollments, they have realized substantial revenue.

Keep Evolving. VUs that are systematically and periodically reexamining their services and funding opportunities are the most successful. Educational technologies are constantly changing, and the VU must evolve along with these changes. For example, many VUs once centrally hosted all of the online courses for their member institutions. As the costs and complexity of course hosting lessened, this typically became a decentralized service. The evolving VU would need to replace this service by addressing other needs of its members that could best be done collectively. The set of collective services is an ever-changing market "basket." As it changes, the funding mechanisms to support new services may also need to be rethought.

The Return of the Private Sector Model. In 2003, Mingle noted the option of using a private sector model. This model often included investments from venture capitalists that would afford developmental funding in anticipation of cashing-in on anticipated profits. During the dot-com boom, several of these private, spin-off entities emerged (such as Cardean University, Virtual Temple, NYUonline). Many of them trumpeted their independence from the traditional institutions that spawned them. When the dot-com bust occurred, there was no safety net and several disappeared. Harvey Stedman, NYU provost, stated that "economic conditions have shifted, and the benefits of having a separate for-profit enterprise have diminished" (Foster, 2007, p. 50).

Over the last several years, private sector funding has not been considered by public VUs. Over that same period, some private institutions (such as the University of Phoenix and Capella University) have enjoyed great success as publicly traded companies with an online education focus. Prior to the 2008 economic crisis, Illinois Global Campus (created by the University of Illinois) and the CSU Global Campus (created by Colorado State University) used a mixture of private and public start-up investments to begin new VUs that were independent from other institutions in their systems. As time goes on, it will be interesting to watch if these entities herald a new financing model or end up being victims of the most recent economic downturn.

As interesting as the private sector economic model may be to consider, the politics of how these new VUs are created is equally as responsible for their success. When NYUonline (and others) expressed interest in creating an independent, for-profit enterprise, it alienated many of the faculty and administrators on existing campuses. There was no political will from the remainder of the university to carry these independent entities through tough economic times. In the past few years, the Illinois Global Campus experienced this tension between administrative independence and faculty governance. Initial plans to create the Global Campus as a for-profit entity free of university regulations eventually gave way to an agreement to form as a nonprofit academic unit of the university (Foster, 2007).

Other semi-independent virtual universities have enjoyed great success. Penn State's World Campus and the University of Maryland University Campus both maintain academic standing while having some autonomy from the campus. The leader of MassachusettsOnline was so successful that he was named the president of the University of Massachusetts, which resulted in an even higher profile for online instruction. Going forward, it remains to be seen whether Illinois Global Campus and CSU Global Campus will have similar success.

The Promise and Threat of Donated Services. A few of the VUs that did not complete the survey stated they could not because the costs of their services were "part of doing business" or were "uncountable." Donated or in-kind services can be the lifeblood of developing VUs, as a team of dedicated individuals breathe life into a new idea.

On the other hand, donated services might be a vulnerability in a VU's financial plan. The Technology Costing Methodology (TCM) is a set

NEW DIRECTIONS FOR HIGHER EDUCATION • DOI: 10.1002/he

of principles and procedures for measuring technology-mediated education costs developed by WCET in concert with the National Center for Higher Education Management Systems (Jones, 2004). TCM stresses the importance of understanding the costs of donated services. Should a change in leadership or priorities occur, the donated services might end and the VU would need to find ways to fund or replace these services.

A handful of VUs no longer exist. Some of them (Rhode Island's WAVERider, Access Arkansas) had very few services and the VU operations were assumed as part of the duties of existing staff. As the number of online courses grew, the ability to sustain their efforts became untenable and the projects were abandoned. Similarly, if a key part of an organization's operational staff or resources are donated, the loss of such an asset could be devastating to the overall service. As with other observations, managing the politics involved with donated services is the key to success.

Virtual University Appropriations Have Not Kept Pace. The VU survey (Michelau and Poulin, 2008) asked for the amount of appropriations for the last three fiscal years (see Table 4). British Columbia's BCcampus, the North Carolina Community College System, and the Utah Education Network had large increases (at least $850,000) from 2005 to 2008. The increases in British Columbia and North Carolina were part of a major ramping up of revised or new entities. For the remainder of the respondents, they reported reductions, appropriations at the same level, or modest increases.

These financial results for U.S. VUs are rather modest considering that this same period was a time of relatively large increases in higher education appropriations in the United States. The National Association of State Budget Officers (2007) reported increases of about 6 to 9 percent in higher education spending between 2005 and 2007. VU appropriations did not seem to participate in this growth to the same extent. Several reasons were offered to explain this outcome; perhaps VUs were no longer a key strategic investment, or they were replacing their appropriations with other income, or VUs had spun off some services to their member institutions.

Given the economic downturn of 2008, government-funded higher education will probably face budget cuts in many states and provinces. VUs can probably also expect cuts in the coming years. With their ability to

Table 4. Year-to-Year Changes in State/Provincial Appropriations

	2005 to 2006	2006 to 2007
Grew	8 (40.0%)	8 (40.0%)
Stayed the same	9 (45.0%)	10 (50.0%)
Reduced	3 (15.0%)	2 (10.0%)

Source: Michelau and Poulin (2008).

create efficiencies and leverage investments, VUs may be valuable tools in overcoming economic hardships.

A Final Word About Politics and Funding

Over the past few years, an alarming number of decisions have been made about the structure and funding of virtual universities as a result of political maneuvering rather than what was the best financial formula for the organization or the institutions they serve. Here are some examples:

- The government's leadership switches parties. The new government does not like the VU created by the old government. They create an organization with a different name and a different leader. A new vision is created, but time is lost during the transition.
- A VU has operated statewide services in an unbiased and effective way. An institution with political clout wants the budget under the VU's control. The legislature moves the service and budget to the institution.
- A new leader is appointed to head the higher education governance structure. A VU is reorganized without a clear plan as to what the new structure or goals will be.
- With lagging government income, funding cuts are implemented across the board. The cut is more devastating to small VUs (which have the ability to leverage efficiencies) than it is to their constituent institutions (which have more leeway in absorbing cuts).

Conclusion

Even though there is no one best financial model, many lessons can be learned from the experiences of VUs. After ten or more years of operations, we know that successful VUs focus on adding value for the institutions and their students. They constantly evolve to meet changing needs. Finally, they monitor state/provincial politics and defend themselves with both data and arguments that prove their contributions to the public.

References

Epper, R. M., and Garn, M. *Virtual College and University Consortia: A National Study.* Boulder, Colo.: State Higher Education Executive Officers, 2003. Retrieved Dec. 16, 2008, from http://wiche.edu/attachment_library/Virtual_College_University.pdf.

Foster, A. *Illinois Plans to Draw 70,000 Students to Distance Education by 2018.* 2007, 53(34). Retrieved Dec. 31, 2008, from http://www.chronicle.com/weekly/v53/i34/34a05001.htm.

Jones, D. *Technology Costing Methodology Handbook, Version 2.0.* Boulder, Colo.: WCET, 2004. Retrieved Dec. 16, 2008, from http://wcet.info/2.0/index.php?q=TCM+Handbook.

Michelau, D. K., and Poulin, R. *Funding of Academic Collaborations.* Boulder, Colo.: Western Interstate Commission for Higher Education, Aug. 2008. Retrieved Dec. 16, 2008, from http://wiche.edu/attachment_library/The_Funding_of_Academic _Collaborations.pdf.

Mingle, J. R. *Organizational and Financing Models for Electronic Consortia: A Review Prepared for the NEON Project of the Western Interstate Commission for Higher Education (WICHE).* Boulder, Colo.: Western Interstate Commission for Higher Education, Sept. 2003.

National Association of State Budget Officers. "Fiscal Year 2006 State Expenditure Report," Fall 2007. Retrieved Dec. 16, 2008, from http://www.nasbo.org/Publications/ PDFs/fy2006er.pdf.

Wolf, D. B., and Johnstone, S. M. "Cleaning up the Language: Establishing a Consistent Vocabulary for Electronically Delivered Academic Programs." *Change, 31*(4), July/August 1999, 34–39.

RUSSELL POULIN *is associate director of WCET (formerly the Western Cooperative for Educational Telecommunications).*

DEMARÉE K. MICHELAU *is director of policy for the Western Interstate Commission for Higher Education (WICHE).*

NEW DIRECTIONS FOR HIGHER EDUCATION • DOI: 10.1002/he

10

Technology can be used to maximize the effectiveness of academic advising for students in virtual institutions.

Academic Advising in a Virtual University

George E. Steele, Karen C. Thurmond

Many institutions are implementing personalized Web-based student services, which will have a profound effect on interacting with students and achieving learning outcomes for students at a distance. We need a new conceptual model for describing the relationship between the advisor and students, as mitigated through use of technology. The model we propose seeks to combine old and new ideas from different fields of study to give a new perspective on academic advising in the virtual education setting.

The need for this new outlook is warranted. Learners in the virtual university may be missing an opportunity for one-on-one ways to connect with a concerned member of the university community (Habley, 2004). We use the term *virtual university* to represent any higher educational institution where a student seeking advising is separated by space or time. Concerned academic advising professionals and faculty advisors search for the right technology and adequate resources to serve these students. Early attempts at academic advising at a distance provided virtual learners with online versions of print resources. However, advisors are going beyond these tools so that all students benefit from the convenience of an integrated portal that includes academic advising, library services, enrollment services, financial services, and other student services.

The National Academic Advising Association (NACADA, 1999) has adapted standards and resources for advising distance learners. NACADA's standards address critical issues and challenges for developing and maintaining advising programs at a distance, including regular evaluation and

New Directions for Higher Education, no. 146, Summer 2009 © Wiley Periodicals, Inc.
Published online in Wiley InterScience (www.interscience.wiley.com) • DOI: 10.1002/he.349

assessment. The Western Cooperative for Educational Telecommunications (WCET), through the Center for Transforming Student Services (CENTSS, n.d.), and the Minnesota State Colleges and Universities (MnSCU) have various resources for identifying best practices for advising distance learners.

Academic advising that takes seriously the need for students to connect with a concerned member of the university community contributes to the success of the student in his or her distance learning; it helps overcome the isolation students often feel while studying at a distance. In a survey of students (Sloan-C, 2006), 17 percent reported that academic advising contributed to an exceptionally positive experience.

We address the possibilities of student services in a virtual university through cognitive processing. We believe that technologies or tools for virtual student services go to the core of defining a model for a new relationship between advising and technology.

A Model for Virtual Advising

Cognitive Processing Models. Our model is based on three models that have cognitive processing implications. The first is Bloom's cognitive taxonomy for learning, one that most advisors are familiar with as educators. The second conceptual model is from the Center for Transforming Student Services (CENTSS) Audits (see Figure 1) and recognizes the growth of student service portals. Implicit in the CENTSS model are various levels of increasing computer capabilities and sophistication. To clarify this implicit relationship, we will use the Data, Information, Knowledge, and Wisdom processing model (DIKW) found in the fields of knowledge management and informational sciences.

The main thrust of our argument is that Web-based student services provide virtual universities with increasingly powerful capabilities that can encourage greater complex cognitive processes for all students. The results of these cognitive processes, such as degree audits or grade point calculations, relieve the user of knowing how to perform these tasks, just as a GPS relieves a user of knowing how to read a map. Results based on complex calculations are produced by technology. These results are presented to students, who may or may not know how the results are produced. A degree audit relieves the user of knowing how courses relate to a program. In both cases, results are produced. As we move to offering student services through a portal, the goal of advising becomes how we reach our students, who are often at a distance, in ways where we can do what is at the core of all advising encounters: to clarify, to probe, to challenge, to support, and to help students develop understanding. By going back to ideas advanced by Bloom (1956), we will be able to draw parallels to the DIKW and CENTSS.

Bloom's Taxonomy. As educators, most academic advisors are familiar with Bloom (1956) and his work on learning taxonomies. Hurt (2007)

Figure 1. Relationship Between Davis and Botkins' Evolution of Computer Capabilities Model and Bloom's Cognitive Domain

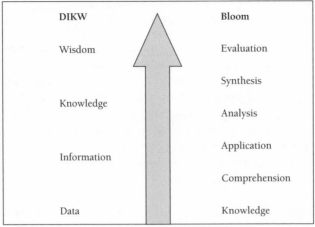

recognized the viability of Bloom's ideas for advisors and suggested that advisors write educational objectives so as to better select tools and guide assessment. The continued application of Bloom's work is a testimony to its value. Bloom (1956) identified three domains of learning: cognitive, affective, and psychomotor. Recently, Bloom's work has been revised by Anderson and Krathwohl (2001). Their revision of Bloom's taxonomy into four general categories of factual, conceptual, procedural, and meta-cognitive knowledge is enlightening and a useful reconceptualization for educators. We use Bloom's original work because it permits a better comparison of the relationships between the CENTSS and the DIKW cognitive processing models. Even though the affective and psychomotor domains are important, we assume that technology plays a critical role in the achievement of cognitive learning.

Bloom (1956) identified six cognitive processing levels in the cognitive domain:

1. *Knowledge:* recall data or information.
2. Comprehension: understand the meaning, translation, interpolation, and interpretation of instructions and problems. States a problem in one's own words.
3. *Application:* use a concept in a new situation or unprompted use of an abstraction. Applies what was learned in the classroom into novel situations in the workplace.
4. *Analysis:* separate material or concepts into component parts so that its organizational structure may be understood. Distinguishes between facts and inferences.

5. *Synthesis:* build a structure or pattern from diverse elements. Puts parts together to form a whole, with emphasis on creating a new meaning or structure.
6. *Evaluation:* make judgments about the value of ideas or materials.

The key point for using Bloom's taxonomy is that it highlights the progression from simple to more complex thought processes. This progression is at the heart of cognitive processing in both the CENTSS and DIKW models.

CENTSS Audits. The CENTSS Audit consists of twenty specialized audits, each focused on assessing specific Web-based student services in an e-learning environment. Examples of audits are financial aid, admissions, academic advising, tutoring, testing, bookstore, career services, course and program catalog, disability services, library services and orientation, communications, counseling, placement, class scheduling, student accounts and activities, registration, and technical support. These Web services can be categorized from zero to four, representing progressively more evolved "generational" levels of technological sophistication. The distinctions among generational levels are due to writing style, personalization and customization of information, number of logins needed to access information, the ability of a student to save personally relevant information, use of specialized tools for planning, and the ability to export relevant data to other personal devices such as a smart phone. In general, the difference between generation one and generation four is the difference between a noninteractive Web page and fully individualized portal services.

To imagine this, consider your online banking experience. What would your experience be if your bank Website had few or no interactive functions and all information was presented on static Web pages, written in language used by accountants and attorneys? These pages would present information about the bank's checking and saving programs. This would be similar to a generation one Website for higher education as defined by the CENTSS audits, written in higher education jargon. Now consider online banking. The information is about *your* accounts. There is a single login. It uses a customer-friendly writing style. Tools help you with financial planning. So if you do online banking, depending on your bank's portal, you have experienced a generation three or four site.

As higher education moves toward greater use of portals, rarely do all twenty of the institution's Web-based student services develop at an equal pace through the levels. In fact, achieving generation four level for all services is probably unobtainable, if not undesirable. The audit tools are to help institutions identify which services may need to be improved, while providing a common language within the institution to facilitate discussion.

Our primary focus is on CENTSS generational levels two and three. These generational levels signify a unique stage in the evolution of technology, which is the difference between Web-based and portal services. Transitioning from generation two to three also represents potential significant

NEW DIRECTIONS FOR HIGHER EDUCATION • DOI: 10.1002/he

change in student cognitive processing. These changes reflect cognitive tasks at the heart of good academic advising.

Evolution of Computer Technology. This section illustrates the relationship between the DIKW model used in information sciences and the generational levels used in the CENTSS model. This highlights critical elements of cognitive processing that advisors should be aware of when assisting students.

The DIKW model is commonly used in the information science and knowledge management fields. DIKW is often referred to as the "Knowledge Hierarchy or Pyramid" or the "Information Hierarchy or Pyramid" (Ackoff, 1989; Sharma, 2008; Zeleny, 1987). The DIKW model has been applied to academic advising (Steele, 2006), as adapted by Davis and Botkins (1994), to focus on how technology affects work processes in an organization. We use it to explain the difference between Web-based and portal-based student services.

The DIKW model has four major stages, comparable to cognitive levels. These stages are data, information, knowledge, and wisdom. For Davis and Botkins, "*education* is instruction and mastery at a given step or level, and *learning* is the movement from one level to the next" (1994, p. 45). At each step up in learning, moving from data to information, information to knowledge, and so on, there is a new technology platform. To illustrate these stages, consider the cognitive process of each stage. For Davis and Botkins (1994), "data are ways of expressing things and information is the arrangement of data into meaningful patterns" (p. 42). Ackoff (1989) considers data as "symbols" and information as processed data that provide answers to "who," "what," "where," and "when" questions. Bellinger, Castro, and Mills (2004) view data simply as a fact, statement, or event without relationship to other information. For our purposes, imagine every field entry in a database as data. This could be an individual course, student's first name, an identification code, or a course identifier. These data become information when combined into patterns such as "all courses available at 8:00 a.m.," "all students who have not registered for a term," or "students who were no-shows for an advising appointment." Another way to imagine this is to view data as parts of speech, such as nouns, verbs, and so forth, and information as sentences. These sentences could answer the questions posed by Ackoff and could be produced as results of a search function.

The last two stages in the DIKW model are knowledge and wisdom: "Knowledge is the application and productive use of information, while wisdom is the discerning use of knowledge" (p. 42). Ackoff (1989) states that knowledge answers "how" questions, while wisdom evaluates understanding. Bellinger, Castro, and Mills (2004) view knowledge as patterns that connect and permit a high level of predictability, while wisdom embodies more of an understanding of fundamental principles.

The DIKW model amounts to a general cognitive processing model. The capabilities of the DIKW model are being shaped by the increased power of computing, as reflected in Moore's Law, which asserts that complexity of a circuit will double about every two years (Moore, 1965). With increased computing power, multiple databases can be easily processed to show relationships not previously considered.

The development of student portals captures higher education's use of technologies within the broad outline of the CENTSS model. In the CENTSS model, at generation two an institution's Website is organized by audience. Categories such as future students, current students, faculty, and alumni are often used to organize the site. Usually the writing is done in an institutional style. The institution's organizational structure is used for the Website design rather than a student or customer perspective. For instance, the site might use "Registrar's Office" rather than "enroll in classes" or "academic advising" rather than "need help." Because the Website is written using the institutional perspective, the information must be interpreted through the lens of the institution. To assist students, forms and e-mail link them with institutional representatives.

At generation three, services of an institution's Website show elements of a personalized portal. The site gives information to the student that is his or her own. This is accomplished because the portal draws on different databases and tables to present the student's personalized information. So rather than seeing the home page of the Registrar's Office, the student accesses his or her past courses and a site to register for the upcoming term or apply for graduation. Rather than seeing a home page of an academic advising office, the student accesses the appointment calendar of an advisor or alternative tools for asking questions. Examples of CENTSS audit items for academic advising in generations two and three are in Figure 2.

We contend that the change from CENTSS generation two to three is parallel to changes in the DIKW stages of information to knowledge. Generation two is parallel to the information stage because it yields a wide assortment of data in a meaningful pattern, which is information. Generation three is parallel to the knowledge stage, for it draws from various sources of information and focuses on an individual student. This quantum leap is critical for understanding implications for advising in this new technology milieu.

The final stage in Davis and Botkins' model is called *wisdom*. Wisdom, the discerning use of knowledge, is a bit more elusive in meaning. Davis and Botkins (1994) argued that technology did not exist to produce wisdom, because wisdom relies on the use of intuition, emotion, and the nonrational. With the use of appropriate tools, a student could pose a question such as, "What if I were to take my Co-op experience spring term rather than autumn term?" Such an inquiry could be considered through a variety of perspectives, including registration, financial aid, or housing. However, this requires a single portal at the generation four level.

Relationship of the CENTSS and DIKW Models to Bloom. The pattern of Bloom's cognitive taxonomy and the DIKW model is illustrated in Figure 3. Both models move from the simplest to the most complex. The highest levels of "wisdom" and "evaluation" are characterized by

Figure 2. Examples of CENTSS Audit Items for Academic Advising for Generations Two and Three

1. Learn about academic offerings, field of study, majors and minors

Generation Two:

Use links for the index or table of contents, or a search tool to find field of study and academic programs. View general information from the online version.

Generation Three:

Use the interactive online catalog. Save links to fields of study and academic programs of interest to My Account. Subscribe to bulletin boards and Webcasts, where I can ask questions of current students, instructors, and career professionals.

2. Run a degree audit

Generation Two:

Fill out an online form requesting a degree audit.

Generation Three:

Log into My Account and run degree audit according to my declared program.

3. Calculate GPA

Generation Two:

Use an online tool to enter grades and calculate GPA.

Generation Three:

Log onto My Account and view my current GPA, enter anticipated grade for current courses to calculate estimated GPA.

value-based judgments and a meta-cognitive characteristic. Both "wisdom" and "evaluation" are highly sought as educational objectives because an awareness of the decision-making process is known by the learner. When focusing on the middle levels, generalizations are a bit more difficult to make, particularly if one wants to draw direct connections. We do not believe direct comparisons at this level should be made. Instead, we note that institutional Websites often list such items as courses to degree requirements or possible careers students can pursue with a specific degree, which are at the "information" level in the DIKW model or the "application level" in Bloom's terminology. While using Bloom's definition of "analysis" and "synthesis," "knowledge" in the DIKW model is transformed in generation three of CENTSS to focus on an individual student. In short, technology is providing the analysis and synthesis of data and information for one

NEW DIRECTIONS FOR HIGHER EDUCATION • DOI: 10.1002/he

Figure 3. Bloom's Taxonomy and DIKW Model

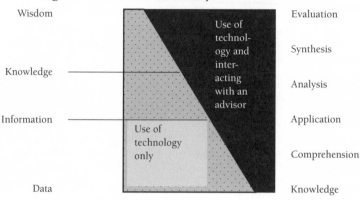

particular student. Degree audits and individual financial aid audits are examples of this analysis and synthesis.

Cautions. For the academic advisor, virtual environments offer an interesting conundrum. On the one hand, the technology can be used by students to acquire a higher level of cognitively processed personalized information. Because these processes are being done by the technology, many students have access to better quality and quantity of information. Ideally, the time advisors and students spend interacting can be focused more on the larger goals of educational and career planning (see Figure 2). On the other hand, this begs several of our initial questions. Students may receive a higher quality and quantity of information to ground their decision making through use of technology, but do they understand it? This might be equivalent to asking advisors or administrators if they understand all the information they have at their disposal from their own online banking portal. Do they trust acting on the personalized financial knowledge acquired through their bank portal? Or do they wish to first see the bank's financial consultant? If financial planning still requires the human touch, academic advising in the virtual environment should also permit some human contact.

Reconceptualizing Technology and Academic Advising. Perhaps the most practical way of showing how these ideas can be implemented is by suggesting adoption of a communication plan for all academic advising services. We offer an admittedly simplistic two-step approach. The first step is to critically review and assess your institution's Website and student portal. The second is to evaluate the suite of communication tools advisors use to assess how effective and efficient they are at facilitating the high-level cognitive interactions needed for students to prepare successful academic and career plans.

NEW DIRECTIONS FOR HIGHER EDUCATION • DOI: 10.1002/he

First, academic advisors must be familiar with the information and tools on the institution's Website and portal. Examples include institutional policies, office contact information, and procedures for making an appointment. These examples are clearly at the informational level of Bloom, or generation one or two in the CENTSS model. Tools such as GPA calculators and degree audits produce knowledge based on an analytical or synthesis level (as described by Bloom) or generation two or three levels (as described by CENTSS). Advisor familiarity with Web information and services cannot stop with his or her own area. The advisor must be prepared to help students with a range of questions that draw on the array of services and information found throughout the institution's Website.

During this period of technology change, different units in the institution may have unequal levels of technological sophistication and adoption. It is not uncommon to see early adopters of technologies in administrative offices such as registration, admissions, and financial aid, while other offices or departments are slower to adopt portal services. But advisors must know what personalized student information is in the student portal. This information will most likely reflect use of technologies that produce a higher level of cognitive production.

The second step is to review the suite of communication tools to which advisors have access. Many issues surround this selection process. Cost, security, harvesting of data exchanges, and examining whether enterprise-level or Web 2.0 solutions are the best course of action are just some of the issues. We urge evaluation of how communications tools supplement interactions with students that can lead to high-level cognitive interactions needed to produce successful academic and career plans. The easiest way to show this is to select and describe four types of tools: e-mail, smart FAQs, telephone, and Web conferencing.

E-mail is one of the most commonly used communication tools used by advisors. E-mail management is one of the biggest headaches encountered by most advisors. There are two main problems with overreliance on e-mail. Some advisors attempt to answer complex higher-order questions, when the tool is designed for shorter informational responses. Second, many advisors attempt to answer the same questions from students, rather than drawing on a store of preanswered responses. These two behaviors hamper the advisor's ability to engage a large number of students in higher-order dialogue.

Smart FAQs refer to an interactive list of frequently asked questions that are one tool in many customer relationship management systems (CRM). The CRM tracks all customer or student interactions, be they e-mail, telephone, smart FAQs, surveys, or Web forms. As with static FAQs, smart FAQs provide a list of commonly asked questions with answers. These responses are at the informational level. But because answers can contain links to other sections of a Website, they can be helpful in guiding students to information and services. Most smart FAQs help students evaluate the effectiveness of the response. New questions and responses based on advisor experience can be developed. This creates a quality feedback loop where answers can be modified and improved on the basis of student suggestions or new questions and responses. Another feature of smart FAQs is a link to e-mail if an answer is not helpful or cannot be found. In this way, an advisor can screen repetitive requests for information and respond to student requests that may require probing questions or moving to another method of interaction to achieve a higher-order dialogue.

The *telephone* remains one of the most effective means of carrying on a dialogue that can produce a higher-order exchange between advisor and student. The ability to use probing questions and listen to the responses is usually far more effective than relying on text-based exchanges. The major drawback is that it is a synchronous tool. Unless phone appointments are made, voice mail exchanges can ensue. Voice mail might be helpful to impart simple information, but these are often lower-level cognitive exchanges.

Web conferencing can include tools that support a very high level of discussion with visual information. Desktop applications such as presentation tools (PowerPoint, Word, Adobe suite), Web browsers, or video conferencing connect advisor and student computers. By using the Web conferencing audio capabilities or a telephone, an advisor can show a student how to use a Website and portal, and show where tools and services are located. More important, the advisor can ask a student through probing questions how the information, tools, and services being reviewed will assist the student in his or her educational and/or career planning. With video conferencing, the advisor can also assess the nonverbal cues. Web conferencing can elevate advising exchanges to a very high level. But like the telephone, it is a synchronous tool and therefore may not offer an immediate response. In addition, it requires a student to have a high-speed Internet connection.

No one tool can be guaranteed to facilitate higher-level cognitive interactions, especially when advising loads are high. These tools need to be part of a system of communication tools that support different types of requests from students. In short, e-mail and smart FAQs should be used to help students with informational requests. If a student needs additional help, such as through a request when a smart FAQ does not address his or her inquiry, telephone and Web conferencing should be used. Using these tools, advisors can help students plan to reach their educational goals.

References

Ackoff, R. "From Data to Wisdom." *Journal of Applied Systems Analysis,* 1989, *16,* 3–9.
Anderson, L. W., and Krathwohl, D. R., eds. *A Taxonomy for Learning, Teaching, and Assessing: A Revision of Bloom's Taxonomy of Educational Objectives.* New York: Longman, 2001.

Bellinger, G., Castro, D., and Mills, A. "Data, Information, Knowledge, and Wisdom," 2004. Retrieved Feb. 3, 2008, from http://www.systems-thinking.org/dikw/dikw.htm.

Bloom, B. *Taxonomy of Educational Objectives, Handbook I: The Cognitive Domain*. New York: David McKay, 1956.

Center for Transforming Student Services (CENTSS). "Beyond the Administrative Core," n.d. Retrieved Dec. 17, 2008, from http://www.wcet.info/services/studentservices/beyond/guidelines/overview.asp#evo.

Davis, S., and Botkins, J. *Monster Under the Bed: How Business Is Mastering the Opportunity of Knowledge for Profit*. New York: Simon and Schuster, 1994.

Habley, W. *Realizing the Potential of Academic Advising*. NACADA Summer Institute on Advising, 2004.

Hurt, R. L. "Advising as Teaching: Establishing Outcomes, Developing Tools, and Assessing Student Learning." *NACADA Journal*, 2007, 27(2), 36–40.

Moore, G. E. "Cramming More Components onto Integrated Circuits." *Electronics Magazine*, 1965. Retrieved Feb. 3, 2008, from http://download.intel.com/museum/Moores_Law/Articles-Press_Releases/Gordon_ Moore_1965_Article.pdf.

National Academic Advising Association. "NACADA Standards for Advising Distance Learners," 1999. Retrieved Nov. 13, 2006, from http://www.nacada.ksu.edu/Clearing house/Research_Related/distance.htm.

Sharma, N. "The Origins of Data, Information, Knowledge, and Wisdom Hierarchy," 2008. Retrieved Aug. 10, 2008, from http://www-personal.si.umich.edu/~nsharma/dikw_origin.htm.

Sloan-C. "Key Practice: Academic and Administrative Services," 2006. Retrieved Nov. 13, 2006, from the Sloan Consortium at http://www.sloan.org/effective/details1.asp?SS_ID=120.

Steele, G. E. "Five Possible Future Work Profiles of Full-Time Academic Advisors." *NACADA Journal*, 2006, 26(2), 48–64.

Zeleny, M. "Management Support Systems: Towards Integrated Knowledge Management." *Human Systems Management*, 1987, 7(7), 59–70.

GEORGE E. STEELE *is director of educational access at the Ohio Learning Network.*

KAREN C. THURMOND *is director of academic advising and a doctoral candidate in higher and adult education at the University of Memphis.*

11

VU leaders stress the importance of strategic planning and understanding online learning as a business.

What to Expect from a Virtual University

Karen Vignare

Virtual universities are designed to make education and educational services accessible and convenient to students for whom a campus based experience does not work.

—*Carol Scarfiotti, vice president emeritus;*
Kishia Brock, dean, Rio Salado College, Arizona

Access Is the Key for Virtual Universities

Virtual universities (VUs) were formed to open up access to higher education for new and existing students, and they continue to grow and thrive. They come in all sizes and organizational and business models, and most differ from their founding institutions. However, VUs face more rigorous requirements for accountability and reporting. Most of those who oversee virtual universities view these requirements as a way toward constant improvement.

This chapter is based on interviews with leaders at the California Virtual Campus, Dallas County Community College District, Empire State College, Governors State, Pennsylvania State University World Campus, Rio Salado College, the Southern Regional Electronic Campus, the Sloan Consortium, and the University of Central Florida. All were asked the same open-ended questions in order to draw on their insights into how and why VUs have become an increasingly important part of public higher education.

The primary reason for the rise of the virtual university is simple. The Internet really did change everything. Some of the pioneers in distance

NEW DIRECTIONS FOR HIGHER EDUCATION, no. 146, Summer 2009 © Wiley Periodicals, Inc.
Published online in Wiley InterScience (www.interscience.wiley.com) • DOI: 10.1002/he.350

education, notably Dallas County Community College's TeleCollege and Penn State University's World Campus, were part of the shift from using the mail for correspondence courses to the Internet. The shift to the Internet allowed the creation of VUs within larger institutions. Though different institutions, both traditional and virtual institutions share a mission of outreach, a core value of virtual universities.

Growth in online enrollment has continued at a rapid pace, though now less than 20 percent per year, which contrasts with total higher education enrollment growth of just over 1 percent a year (Allen and Seaman, 2007). These students include adults and those currently enrolled. All those interviewed agreed that VU enrollment growth would continue to outpace growth of traditional institutions. In states such as California, where adding new buildings in tight budget times is unthinkable, the California Virtual Campus is experiencing 10 percent growth in enrollment.

> We [CVC] fully expect, particularly if we head into a recession here for the next five years or so, that eighteen-to-twenty-two-year-olds will take more online courses—students may have to work more to get through school, and loans may be much harder to get— fewer students will have the luxury of full-time studenthood.
>
> —*Doug Cremer, executive director, California Virtual Campus*

The growth in traditional-aged college students enrolling in online learning is a result of several trends, including the growth in online associate and bachelor's degree programs. Also, many high school students are taking high school and college courses online (Picciano and Seaman, 2007). Almost seven hundred thousand high school students are taking online courses at a growing number of virtual high schools.

Integrating Services, Faculty, and Space for Maximum Efficiency

The shift to these new learners has created challenges for VUs. An integrated VU such as the University of Central Florida (UCF) serves the spectrum of students and faculty who choose to participate in blended or online learning. UCF's distributed approach avoids past mistakes, according to Joel Hartman, vice-provost for information technology and resources:

> Most virtual universities that have failed in the past had the following common characteristics: administrators who got far ahead of their faculty, overoptimistic estimates of demand, and underestimates of cost. Success comes from three levels: administrative vision aligned with institutional goals, willing faculty, and midlevel units capable of facilitation and assessment.

The State University of New York, through its creation of the SUNY Learning Network, was one of the first states systems to adopt a statewide approach successfully. VUs can expect states to continue to demand that institutions share resources across a system. One of the problems is that new investment for instructional design support, new technologies, online student services, and access to libraries is needed. Hartman shared this about the successful planning of their virtual university:

> The University of Central Florida's Online@UCF initiative is an example of a mature program that can demonstrate a positive return on investment. In addition to providing the university with expanded instructional capacity that would today cost $36 million to construct and nearly $2 million a year to operate, the initiative generates just over $17 for each dollar of direct expenditure, not including instructional costs.

Recognize Bureaucratic and Outdated Public Policy

Policies on accountability, accreditation, quality, and access contribute to more virtual universities starting at the institutional or state level. Once begun, the VU must make its virtual operations align with all academic processes of the university or state system. Fortunately, regional accreditors have coalesced around best practices and guidelines for distance learning (Council of Regional Accrediting Commissions, 2001), but there may still be regulation from institutional, system, or state offices.

Public higher education could use assistance from government, regulators, and regional accreditors to run more successful VUs. Bruce Chaloux, president of the Sloan Consortium and director for the Southern Regional Electronic Campus, offers a list of how public policymakers could help:

1. Change the funding models away from the traditional campus-based approaches; do away with in-state versus out-of-state tuition rates.
2. Allow, indeed promote, a true competency-based learning model that rewards students (with credits) for demonstrated knowledge rather than time spent in a seat.
3. Encourage, through more open credit transfer, recognition of the academic coin of the realm (credits), which would recognize that students take courses from multiple providers; allow them to "bank" credits for application toward degrees.
4. Create a nationwide accreditation system (not operated by the federal government) that would remove the barriers for many virtual institutions operating in multiple states.

There Is No Best Business Model

Controversy continues on the best business model for VUs. Three models from the past decade seem to predominate: cost or profit center (requires that the unit make a profit or pay back the money it uses), overhead/service center (the unit is given funds from the general fund), and independent for-profit model (allows the VU to be a separate entity and run like a for-profit business; Geith, Schiffman, and Vignare, 2005). Pennsylvania World Campus shifted from being a profit center to a service center. The business model also dictates how the VU operates within the larger university. Operations can be centralized, decentralized, or a combination. Centralized operations require the VU to work with other departments to determine services and agreements. However, if the VU is not a priority, its requests are not filled promptly, hampering the VU's effectiveness. Decentralized models allow the VU to create its own services or buy them from another department. This encourages creativity and quicker resolution of technology and service problems, but it may lead to development of duplicative services.

Online Students Want Control and Convenience

The rise of VUs has truly opened doors for students. Students now have a choice of what kind of learning experience they get, whether online, in a traditional classroom, or blended where the two methods are mixed. Recent surveys (Dziuban, Moskal, Brody, and Shea, 2007; Salaway, Caruso, and Nelson, 2008) show students find that online courses offer convenience, flexibility, and control. Those who feel inhibited in the face-to-face setting experience more interaction. Yet a few students remain dissatisfied and ambivalent about the experience.

Many public VUs do not track students in online programs. Rio Salado College uses a customer relationship management system that is also employed by for-profits to make sure all online student interactions are tracked and measured. This tracking is not just about making sure students get what they need (advising, tutoring, registration); it also ensures these services are continuously improved to meet changing student needs. Successful public and for-profit VUs provide students with services around the clock and offer flexibility as to when students begin courses. Thus, places such as Rio Salado College and Empire State are experimenting with offering courses that run six to eight weeks and no longer fit into the traditional fall, spring, and summer academic calendar.

From the late 1990s to 2008, for-profit VUs grew from serving 3 percent of all individuals attending higher education to over 8 percent. Public higher education competitors are also growing rapidly, such as Empire State in New York. Empire State serves adults and has rapidly changed to support the growth of virtual education. Yet at least one expert feels that for-profits will face more competition from public higher education.

> For-profit companies that offer degrees online were a response to a market need. The current workforce needed to get a fresh education in order to compete in a globalizing economy. However,

as more traditional universities enter the field, for-profits will have increasing difficulty competing for new students.

—Gary Miller, executive director emeritus,
Penn State World Campus

How institutions treat students is critical. Usage of student services is tracked, allowing for-profits to add service where needed and move staff if services are not in demand. This centralized approach promotes accessibility and predictability for students. Reliable online student services have been a key recommendation for VUs from policy leaders such as Western Cooperative for Educational Telecommunications (WCET) since 2000.

So regardless of the VU type (stand-alone or integrated), students need a comprehensive set of services. For the future, these services will become increasingly important because students can easily leave and attend another institution. Students are also likely to continue to expect that all services will be available online and anytime.

Faculty Pedagogy and Instructional Training Needed

In the traditional university, faculty could do basically what they wanted to in the confines of the classroom. Since it was difficult to measure success or really "see" and know what was happening, faculty had a tremendous amount of autonomy. In the virtual world, classes can be seen. Interaction measured. Quality can be better measured. Consistent content can be used. Faculty become more of a facilitator.

—Pam Quinn, provost, Dallas TeleLearning,
Dallas County Community College District

The process of going online is difficult for both faculty and the institution. According to the Sloan-C pillars, faculty need technical support, quality control of their courses, institutional rewards, and some administrative control. Faculty also want research resulting from online learning to be considered valuable and enjoy the new access to students from online interactive learning communities (Moore, 2005). Research into faculty satisfaction indicates that it is tied to two things: choice and preparedness. Faculty who are required, rather than choose, to teach online are more reluctant to redesign courses. Faculty who are given instructional support and preparation time to learn how to teach online indicate they are more satisfied with their online teaching experience (Dziuban and others, 2004; Shea, Pickett, and Pelz, 2003). Case study research on faculty also point to a high level of satisfaction when faculty feel that their teaching strategies have had a positive impact on students (Moore, Sener, and Fetzner, 2006). Evidence that online or blended learning meets student needs for flexibility and addresses multiple learning styles also increases faculty satisfaction (Shea, Pickett, and Pelz, 2003).

Pioneers such as University of Central Florida have created a distributed support system where all faculty, those teaching partially or wholly online, can receive the same training. Training at the University of Maryland University College is free to faculty teaching a course (Bishop and SchWeber, 2002). Even for-profits such as University of Phoenix require training for first-time faculty and insist on continuing professional development for adjuncts (Trippe, 2002). Training varies greatly in some institutions, from how to use basic technology tools to effective pedagogical techniques (Arabasz and Baker, 2003). However, all institutions struggle to get faculty to come to training (Hitt and Hartman, 2002; Otte, 2005).

Many faculty who teach online go on to be champions of online learning. These "early adopters" often serve as mentors for faculty new to online learning. Yet some faculty act as barriers, with many facing other pressures on their time. At research institutions they are pushed to find grants and publish. For them to be successful, a VU will need to consider how to change the tenure and reward system. Yet those working at both doctoral and traditional institutions represent only a portion of the faculty teaching online. Many institutions increasingly rely on part-time and adjunct faculty, who may have more or less interest in learning how to teach online or to prepare online courses.

Instructional support or instructional design, academic support, teaching and learning support, faculty development, educational technologies, and instructional technologies are another necessary component for a VU. Many faculty are hired to be content experts and are not taught how to teach, and teaching in a virtual environment requires more planning and preparation. All faculty need help from instructional designers to decide which teaching strategies will work best for the course content. Furthermore, if a VU plans to be cost-effective, it should create courses where the content can be shared. These courses are often referred to as master courses and should be designed by faculty recognized as subject matter experts and an instructional team of designers and technologists. The process is not cheap, but because the course can be used by multiple sections of the course and many other faculty, the investment pays off over time (Twigg, 2003).

With the master course built, the focus is now placed on the online environment. The most popular model for designing online courses is the Community of Inquiry model (Garrison, Anderson, and Archer, 2000). The model helps faculty and instructional designers understand the importance of three activities, called teaching, cognitive, and social presence. Student survey data lend clear evidence that planning instruction using such a model is critical for online students (Swan and others, 2008). The model can be applied regardless of whether a course is designed by a team or one faculty member. Once courses are designed, VUs can spend more time with faculty improving the online learning experience for students.

Sophisticated Marketing and Research Required

Perhaps one of the largest differences between for-profit and public higher education is development of degrees. By using marketing research, for-profits offer degrees that appeal to more online-learning students. Academics in traditional universities often dictate whether a program or degree is offered. In the future, VUs must create a more collaborative climate for strategic planning, where marketing researchers, admissions experts, and academics work together to ensure student success. This strategic alliance does not stop at which degrees are planned but should continue through student completion so that improvement in courses and student services can be continuous.

The focus of marketing now is making sure the right student—one who is ready to learn—enrolls. However, VUs must also keep students engaged while pursuing their degree. Penn State's World Campus has hired a social networks advisor to keep students active and engaged in multiple student communities, including Second Life and Facebook. These new tools also serve in internal and external marketing to potential students.

The Future Virtual University Will Integrate Services

From the interviews, it is clear that whether the VU started as independent or centralized, leaders would recommend an integrated and strategic approach to planning. State and public higher education players expect VUs to grow and serve a more diverse set of students. However, the strategic planning and cultural changes required for a successful VU take time and should not be shortchanged. Good planning information is available from accreditation agencies, distance learning and educational technology associations, successful virtual universities, and publications such as this one. John Stoll, vice provost at Governors State University, offers these final words of advice to those launching virtual universities:

- Traditional student services must be available for students who never come to campus.
- Seat time must be rethought as a measure of success.
- The virtual university's needs must be incorporated into the processes for curriculum development and engagement of full-time faculty.
- Business processes connecting to students (and frankly to faculty who may not be on campus as frequently) must be modified to support the needs of those who cannot come to the cashier's window.
- There is a need to create online student community beyond the classroom.

The clear preference among the early virtual university leaders interviewed is to integrate the VU within a larger college or university. This is odd because many VUs had to be protected from the host university when they started, or they were established as an independent entity. It is important to remember that methods for incubating a new process, service, or product are not new and have been studied in other settings. However, it is clear that the biggest challenge is deciding on whether a VU should be separate or not. For example, even though a separate and independent virtual university focuses more on being financially successful, a VU integrated within a larger university shares the substantial cost of putting courses and services online. In any case, the decision to initiate a virtual university must be tailored to the needs, culture, and resources of the hosting institution in light of what we currently know about virtual universities, which is likely to evolve as more research is done.

References

Allen, E., and Seaman, J. *Online Nation: Five Years of Growth in Online Learning.* Needham, Mass.: Sloan Consortium, 2007.

Arabasz, P., and Baker, M. B. (2003). Supporting E-Learning in Higher Education. *EDUCAUSE Center for Applied Research.* Retrieved Mar. 23, 2009, from http://www.educause.edu/ers0303/1786.

Bishop, T., and SchWeber, C. "Link Cost to Quality." In J. Bourne and J. Moore (eds.), *Elements of Quality Online Education, 3* (pp. 45–58). Needham, Mass.: Sloan-C, 2002.

Council of Regional Accrediting Commissions. "Best Practices for Electronically Offered Degree and Certificate Programs," 2001. Retrieved Dec. 15, 2008, from http://wcet.info/resources/accreditation/Accrediting%20-%20Best%20Practices.pdf.

Dziuban, C., Hartman, J., Moskal, P., Sorg, S., and Truman, B. "Three ALN Modalities: An Institutional Perspective." In J. Bourne and J. Moore (eds.), *Elements of Quality Online Education: Into the Mainstream* (pp. 127–148). Needham, Mass.: Sloan-C, 2004.

Dziuban, C., Moskal, P., Brody, J., and Shea, P. "Student Satisfaction with Asynchronous Learning." *Journal of Asynchronous Learning Networks,* 2007, *11*(1), 87–95.

Garrison, D. R., Anderson, T., and Archer, W. "Critical Inquiry in a Text-Based Environment: Computer Conferencing in Higher Education." *Internet and Higher Education,* 2000, *2*(2–3), 87–105.

Geith, C., Schiffman, S., and Vignare K. "Identifying Successful Business Strategies for Distance Learning." *Sloan Consortium View,* 2005, *4*(6). Retrieved Dec. 22, 2008, from http://www.sloan-c.org/publications/view/v4n6/bizstrat.htm.

Hitt, J. C., and Hartman, J. L. *Distributed Learning: New Challenges and Opportunities for Institutional Leadership.* Washington, D.C.: American Council on Education, Center for Policy Analysis, 2002.

Moore, J. "A Synthesis of Sloan-C Effective Practices." *Journal of Asynchronous Learning Networks,* 2005, *9*(3), 55–73.

Moore, J., Sener, J., and Fetzner, M. "Getting Better: ALN and Student Success." *Journal of Asynchronous Learning Networks,* 2006, *10*(3), 55–84.

Otte, G. "Using Blended Learning to Drive Faculty Development (and Vice Versa)." In J. Bourne and J. Moore (eds.), *Elements of Quality Online Education: Engaging Communities* (pp. 71–83). Needham, Mass.: Sloan-C, 2005.

Picciano, A., and Seaman, J. "K–12 Online Learning: A Survey of U.S. School District Administrators." Needham, Mass.: Sloan Consortium, 2007.

Salaway, G., Caruso, J., and Nelson, M. "The ECAR Study of Undergraduate Students and Information Technology" (Research Study, Vol. 8). Boulder, Colo.: EDUCAUSE Center for Applied Research, 2008. Retrieved Dec. 22, 2008, from http://www.educause.edu/ecar.

Shea, P., Pickett, A., and Pelz, W. "A Follow up Investigation of 'Teacher Presence' in the SUNY Learning Network." *Journal of Asynchronous Learning Networks,* 2003, 7(2), 61–80.

Swan, K., and others. "Validating a Measurement Tool of Presence in Online Communities of Inquiry." *e-mentor,* 2008, 2(24). Retrieved Dec. 22, 2008, from http://www.e-mentor.edu.pl/artykul_v2.php?numer=24&id=543.

Trippe, A. "Student Satisfaction at the University of Phoenix Online Campus." In J. Bourne and J. Moore (eds.), *Elements of Quality Online Education,* 3 (pp. 45–58). Needham, Mass.: Sloan-C, 2002.

Twigg, C. "Improving Learning and Reducing Costs: New Models for Online Learning." *Educause Review,* Sept. /Oct. 2003, 28–38. Retrieved Dec. 22, 2008, from http://connect.educause.edu/Library/EDUCAUSE+Review/ImprovingLearningandReduc/40427.

Karen Vignare is director of customer experience at MSU (Michigan State University) Global Campus.

New Directions for Higher Education • DOI: 10.1002/he

12

Many research questions about virtual universities need answers.

What We Need to Know About Virtual Universities

Katrina A. Meyer

The previous chapters have presented glimpses of what we know about virtual universities. Certainly, they seem to use a number of organizational models, offer different services, and were founded to achieve a variety of aims. We know they use various funding models, are successful or not to differing degrees, and may have encouraged the development of online learning and services within other institutions in the state. In other words, we still know little about these new types of higher education. This chapter reviews only the most obvious questions raised by the work of our authors and leaves the development of more intricate questions to a future generation of researchers.

The chapter summarizing the Epper and Garn study begs for answers to several questions. If the study were duplicated today, what would be the results? Would there be more VUs or fewer, and would they be more variable or less? Would organizational structures be more consistent or less? What is happening among VUs that are not aligned to state systems? Are for-profit or independent VUs very different from the public models, and what can public VUs learn from these models? What can we learn from comparing the development and characteristics of VUs in the United States with models developed in other countries? What lessons can we learn from other national or multinational VUs?

The chapter on definitions and new taxonomies for virtual universities leaves us wondering whether these taxonomies continue to capture useful distinctions; or do we need new taxonomies or modified versions of these earlier ones? Is there more variation among types or less? Have some types

New Directions for Higher Education, no. 146, Summer 2009 © Wiley Periodicals, Inc.
Published online in Wiley InterScience (www.interscience.wiley.com) • DOI: 10.1002/he.351

of new institutions become popular and others less so? Or have virtual institutions lost their distinctive differences, and if so, why would this have happened?

After reading the chapters on WashingtonOnline and Georgia's eCore, you may see some obvious questions about whether the virtual experience is substantially different or more effective for students taking online courses at community colleges or in general education. Certainly, the research literature on student learning in online settings is growing, but is there any evidence that the organizational or development model—exemplified by the two models in Washington and Georgia—has any impact on student learning? How well do students who get their associate of arts or their first two years of coursework done online perform at four-year institutions or later in their lives? As for organizational questions, will WAOL or other centralized organizations continue to offer new and different services, and what will they be? Will campuses continue the process of adopting and providing services once offered by a central body?

How has the faculty development services offered by these virtual universities affected the faculty's pedagogical skills, and have these new skills changed what happens when these faculty return to face-to-face classrooms? In fact, are faculty involved in VUs somehow different from those in traditional institutions, or are they largely the same individuals? How have the changes in faculty roles brought about by new higher education arrangements such as VUs affected faculty careers? Will eCore solve its scalability problem, and how? Can it learn some tips from other large providers, or is scalability of services and instruction something that can only be resolved idiosyncratically, by each state or system? There must be general principles to scalability, but what are they? To solve the problem of scalability, how will organizations address distributed responsibilities (as our authors put it: when something is everyone's job, it is no one's job) or the critical (and unscalable) role of personal relationships to smooth collaboration across campuses? Have these new structures and ways of doing business been more cost-efficient?

Western Governors University leaves us with even more open questions. We need to know more about WGU's cost structures and its cost per student or assessment. We need much more information about how effective it has been, and what those who lead WGU have learned through the process of breaking so many molds. What would they recommend as being cost-effective practices to other institutions? What would they not do again? Finally, although this would be an enormous undertaking, we need to evaluate the WGU model against the model it dropped during its early development stage: the brokering model, where courses from institutions were shared among students and institutions. To do this, one could compare WGU to the Electronic Campus, the Southern Regional Education Board's effort at brokering and coordinating online education in the southern states.

A comparison of these two models would highlight how choice of policies and practices affects each organization's current success, or identify the advantages and disadvantages of policy choices.

Chapters Six and Seven compared sets of VUs and generated a host of research questions. When do centralized organizations work, and when do decentralized organizations? Is it a matter of culture, or are some types of decisions better made at the campus level and others at the central office? Is there an optimal leadership style or theory for consortial arrangements such as these, or are there multiple approaches that succeed? What are the strengths and weaknesses of consortia, or are they influenced by idiosyncracies of the state or system? Although Xu and Morris conclude that VUs may work best when higher education institutions are made the organization's customers rather than students, are there exceptions? Garn proposes an intriguing question: What evidence is there that virtual universities transformed the traditional institutions in the state? Clearly, we need to monitor change among VUs; these two chapters indicate that VUs have changed in both major and minor ways over their short lifetimes. We also need many more comparison studies of statewide VUs to enlighten us on the effect of organizational models, practices, philosophies, and policies.

But Chapter Eight, on the short life of the U.S. Open University, also makes clear that we need many more studies of virtual organizations—be they for profit or nonprofit—that have failed. We learn as much or more from our failures as from our successes, and this would be a very fruitful area for future researchers. Why did these failures happen? Did they occur as a result of wrong assumptions, poor execution, loss of critical leadership, or changing dynamics? Does the choice of programs to offer have an impact on the success of the VU? Are large-enrollment or widely popular programs the only way a VU can garner the enrollments it needs to survive and thrive, and what might this imply for the availability of smaller, more boutique online programs that appeal to a smaller number of students? What can we learn about failures to ensure new higher education organizations avoid such mistakes?

The chapter on funding of virtual organizations is equally enlightening and leaves us asking more questions. Given the current economic downturn, what will happen to virtual universities? Will the proportions of funding from the state/province, students, and private sources shift, and what will this mean for VUs? What happens when the organization has only one funding source? This chapter also raised issues of scalability and staffing, and whether VUs funded on a shoestring, using existing staff and resources, are fated for failure, and if not, what saved them from failing? Finally, are some funding structures more cost-efficient or successful than others?

Chapter Ten presented a model for new online student services, using academic advising as an example. As we implement portal systems on campuses and VUs, will they be able to generate the complex cognitive processes among students that the authors propose? Clearly, the model needs to be tested and perhaps refined, and then applied to other essential online student services. There also needs to be much more research on online student services generally, to ascertain their impact on student learning and development.

Chapter Eleven tapped the experiences of VU leaders, but it leaves us wondering whether their advice will remain valid as VUs continue to change. Or is new advice needed to cover all kinds of situations that VUs face in a rapidly changing funding and competitive environment? Will new models or solutions become the way VUs should operate? Or will the advice of our VU leaders have legs?

Clearly, VUs are fascinating and novel higher education organizations. They disprove the old saw that change in higher education happens at a glacial pace, and they prove that innovation is alive and well in public higher education. VUs have innovated with new organizational structures, new collaboration models, new delivery modes, new policies, new assessment models, new funding models, and new skills on the part of students, faculty, and administrators. Yet we still need to understand how well these innovations are doing and whether they produce unintended consequences we cannot see at present. We need to see beyond the immediate state of enrollments to how VUs may be affecting more traditional institutions. We need to learn as much as we can from these organizations so that good innovations can be adopted more widely and failures be avoided. It will be up to thoughtful practitioners at VUs to study what they are doing and share their insights, as well as academic researchers to study these institutions in more detail in order to find the jewels and avoid the stones. The future of higher education may depend on what we learn.

KATRINA A. MEYER *is associate professor of higher and adult education at the University of Memphis.*

NEW DIRECTIONS FOR HIGHER EDUCATION • DOI: 10.1002/he

INDEX

Jarvis, R., 67
Johnson, M. J., 46
Johnstone, S. M., 7, 13, 46, 74
Jones, D., 82

Kennedy, T., 46
Kentucky, 49; Council on Postsecondary Education (CPE), 59; Department of Adult Education, 60; Distance Learning Advisory Committee (DLAC), 59; Education Professional Standards Board, 60; General Assembly, 59, 61
Kentucky Commonwealth Virtual University, 59
Kentucky Community and Technical College System (KCTCS), 59, 60
Kentucky Virtual Campus, 77
Kentucky Virtual Library, 59–60
Kentucky Virtual University (KYVU), 47–49, 56, 59–63; organizational structure, 48; reasons for lack of participation in, 48–49; services, 48
Keynes, Milton, 65
King, J. W., 46
Kinser, K., 36
"Knowledge Hierarchy or Pyramid," 89
Kozoll, C. E., 33
Krathwohl, D. R, 87
Krenelka, L. M., 65–68, 70

Lasseter, M. R., 26, 32
Leavitt, M. (Utah governor), 37
Lee, K., 32
Lippitt, G. L., 36
Loader, B. D., 46
Lozier, G., 59–60

Martineau, L. P., 35
MassachusettsOnline, 81
McCoy, D. R., 35, 46
McDonald's University, 12
Merriam, S. B., 46
Meyer, K. A., 11, 36, 39, 65, 67, 107
Michelau, D. K., 73, 76
Michigan: K-12 community, 61, 63; legislature, 58; Presidents Council, 58; Teacher and Technology Initiative, 59
Michigan Association of Secondary School Administrators, 58–59
Michigan Community College Association Virtual Learning Collaborative, 58
Michigan Education Association, 58–59
Michigan Virtual Automotive College, 58
Michigan Virtual High School (MVHS), 58, 62
Michigan Virtual Technology College, 58

Michigan Virtual University (MVU), 56, 58, 59, 61–63
Middle States Association of Colleges and Schools, 67
Miller, G., 100–101
Miller, J. W., 35
Mills, A., 89
Mingle, J. R., 74, 79
Minnesota State Colleges and Universities eFolio, 77
Moore, G. E., 89–90
Moore, J., 101
Moore, M. G., 46
Moore's Law, 89–90
Morris, L. V., 28, 31, 32, 45, 109
Moskal, P., 100, 101
Motorola University, 12
Multi-institutional functionality, 29

National Academic Advising Association (NACADA), 85
National Association of State Budget Officers, 82
National Center for Educational Statistics, 45
National Center for Higher Education Management Systems (NCHEMS), 62
National Technology University, 12
Native Americans, 22
Nelson, M., 100
NETg, 58
No Child Left Behind, 59, 62
NYUonline, 81

Oblinger, D., 55, 59–60
Ohio, 49
Ohio Learning Network (OLN), 47; barriers and challenges to, 50; organizational structure of, 49; positive aspects of, 50; services, 49–50
Olcott, D., 46
Oliver, C., 27
Olympia, Washington, 22
Online learning, statewide administration models: and California Virtual University (CVU), 56–57; and Florida Virtual Campus, 57–58; and Kentucky Virtual University (KYVU), 59–60; and Michigan Virtual University, 58–59
Oracle, 57
Oracle Internet Academies, 58
Otte, G., 102

Pacific Bell, 57
Patton, Paul E. (Kentucky governor), 59, 62

marketing online offerings in national market with limited funds, 68

UT TeleCampus (UTTC; University of Texas), 47, 50; Academic Affairs Committee, 51; barriers and challenges faced by, 52; Executive Committee, 51; organizational structure of, 50–51; positive aspects of, 51–52; services, 51

Utah, 36, 37; Education Network, 78

UTTC, 50–52.

Valdosta State University (Georgia), 26

Vignare, K., 97, 100

Virtual advising: and Bloom's taxonomy, 87–88; cautions for, 92; and CNTSS Audit, 88–89; and cognitive processing models, 86–87; and evolution of computer technology, 89–90; model for, 86–94; reconceptualizing technology and, 92–94

Virtual colleges and universities (VCU): comparison of organizational models of, 7–8; lessons learned from Epper and Garn study on, 8–9; overview of, in 2002, 5–7

Virtual franchises, 32

Virtual Institution Design Team (Florida), 57

Virtual institutions, 14

Virtual organization with place-bound offerings, 14

Virtual Temple, 81

Virtual universities: access as key for, 97–98; and control and convenience for online students, 100–101; four models of, 14–15; and integrated services, 103–104; integrating services, faculty, and space for maximum efficiency in, 98–99; lack of best business model for, 99–100; need for faculty pedagogy and instructional training in, 101–102; and need for sophisticated marketing and research, 103; and new definitions for new higher education institutions, 11–15; and recognizing bureaucratic and outdated policy, 99; seven organizational models for, 11–13; two new institutional taxonomies for, 13–14; what needs to be known about, 107–110; what to expect from, 97–110

Virtual universities, funding of, 73–83; and annual budget of virtual university central administrative units, 76t;

and diversifying funding sources, 79–80; and number of funding sources, 79t; observations and conclusions about, 78–79; and organizational and funding taxonomies, 74–75; sources for, 76–77

Washington, D.C., 55

Washington State, 17, 108

Washington State Board for Community and Technical Colleges, 20–22

Washington State Community and Technical Colleges, 20

WashingtonOnline: background and history of, 17–19; and comparison of annualized student FTE supported by WAOL and WAOL staff FTE, 18; as consortium, 17; cost model, 21; faculty and staff professional development, 23; focus on student learning, 21–23; functioning of, 19; lessons learned from, 17–24; and over- and undercommunication, 23–24; and shared course development, 20–21; system technology plan, 21

Western Cooperative for Educational Telecommunications (WCET), 36, 76, 86, 101

Western Governors Association, 55

Western Governors University (WGU), 11, 12, 15, 33, 45, 47, 55, 57, 60, 108; breaking mold at, 35–36; changes and redirections at, 36–42; changing mission of, 38–39; experiencing innovation at, 41–42; issues at, 42; multiple objectives of, 40–41; organizational models for, 38; and politics, 37–38; in present, 42

Western Interstate Commission for Higher Education (WICHE), 76

Williams, J. B., 31

Wilmington, Delaware, 66

Wilson, P. (California governor), 56, 57, 61–63

Wolf, D. B., 7, 13, 46, 74

Wong, A., 31

Wu, S., 31

Xu, H., 28, 32, 45, 109

Yin, R. K., 46

Zeleny, M., 89

NEW DIRECTIONS FOR HIGHER EDUCATION

ORDER FORM SUBSCRIPTION AND SINGLE ISSUES

DISCOUNTED BACK ISSUES:

Use this form to receive 20% off all back issues of *New Directions for Higher Education*.
All single issues priced at **$23.20** (normally $29.00)

TITLE	ISSUE NO.	ISBN
_____	_____	_____
_____	_____	_____
_____	_____	_____

*Call 888-378-2537 or see mailing instructions below. When calling, mention the promotional code JB9ND
to receive your discount. For a complete list of issues, please visit www.josseybass.com/go/ndhe*

SUBSCRIPTIONS: (1 YEAR, 4 ISSUES)

☐ New Order   ☐ Renewal

U.S.	☐ Individual: $89	☐ Institutional: $228
CANADA/MEXICO	☐ Individual: $89	☐ Institutional: $268
ALL OTHERS	☐ Individual: $113	☐ Institutional: $302

*Call 888-378-2537 or see mailing and pricing instructions below.
Online subscriptions are available at www.interscience.wiley.com*

ORDER TOTALS:

Issue / Subscription Amount: $ _____

Shipping Amount: $ _____
(for single issues only – subscription prices include shipping)

Total Amount: $ _____

SHIPPING CHARGES:

First Item	$5.00
Each Add'l Item	$3.00

*(No sales tax for U.S. subscriptions. Canadian residents, add GST for subscription orders. Individual rate subscriptions must
be paid by personal check or credit card. Individual rate subscriptions may not be resold as library copies.)*

BILLING & SHIPPING INFORMATION:

☐ **PAYMENT ENCLOSED:** *(U.S. check or money order only. All payments must be in U.S. dollars.)*

☐ **CREDIT CARD:** ☐ VISA ☐ MC ☐ AMEX

Card number _____ Exp. Date _____

Card Holder Name _____ Card Issue # _____

Signature _____ Day Phone _____

☐ **BILL ME:** *(U.S. institutional orders only. Purchase order required.)*

Purchase order # _____
Federal Tax ID 13559302 • GST 89102-8052

Name _____

Address _____

Phone _____ E-mail _____

Copy or detach page and send to: **John Wiley & Sons, PTSC, 5th Floor
989 Market Street, San Francisco, CA 94103-1741**

Order Form can also be faxed to: **888-481-2665**

PROMO JB9ND